"In *Daily Decrees for Accessing Abundance*, Joshua Fowler has written an excellent book on the value, power, and practical uses of daily decrees. Discover how you can use Scripture to open doors of abundance and favor in every area of your life. Joshua has managed to combine scholarly wisdom, spiritual power, and practical direction into an easy-to-read format that can be useful to believers of all ages. Read, apply, and move into a greater level of abundance today!"

—*Joan Hunter*
Author, evangelist, and president of Joan Hunter Ministries

"In John 1:1 we read, '*In the beginning was the Word.*' In other words, before the beginning there was something that existed. That something was the Word. Before anything begins in your life it needs a word in order to have the right to begin. In *Daily Decrees for Accessing Abundance*, Joshua Fowler has written a clear and precise guide to help us unlock resources and treasures of the kingdom like never before. If you know there are things being 'held back' from you in life, this book you hold is a must-read!"

—*Bishop Gary Oliver*
Tabernacle of Praise, Fort Worth, TX

"Do you like the world around you? If not, change it by decreeing God's Word until a positive kingdom environment is created. Dr. Joshua Fowler has tapped into the understanding of God's wisdom that is concealed in the biblical principle of Job 22:28. When the Word of God is decreed in faith, it releases the ingenious power of revelation knowledge so that profound mysteries can be revealed and manifested as covenant blessings. Dr. Fowler's new book will equip you to move into the dimension of success to obtain your destiny."

—*Dr. Barbie L. Breathitt*
Certified Dream Life Coach, Breath of the Spirit Ministries
Author, *A to Z Dream Symbology Dictionary* and *Dream Encounters*

"*Daily Decrees for Accessing Abundance* is a God-Word from an apostolic general who carries a mighty mantle to equip believers to live an extraordinary life in the kingdom! Apostle Fowler has tapped into a powerful revelation to cause *increase* and *restoration* in your life. This divine word from heaven shall cause your spirit to soar. As you put into practice daily this word from the Holy Spirit, you will see dramatic changes in your life and future. This mighty man of God has spent much time in His presence in order to cause a great impartation into your life!"

—*Dr. Coy Barker*
Founder, Elevation Point, Loganville, GA
coybarker.com
ElevationPoint.org

"*Daily Decrees for Accessing Abundance* offers an impressive and practical way to apply the power of decreeing God's Word. This book will boost your faith to believe and receive from the abundant supply that flows from the throne of God to every believer."

—*Steven J. Gray*
Pastor, World Revival Church of Kansas City

"Joshua Fowler is one of the most prophetic voices of our generation. The principles and revelation in this book have the potential to produce a significant shift in your life and your family. Joshua teaches you how to make powerful decrees that will cause your God-given destiny to find you and bring you the resources you need to accomplish your assignment. This book will equip you to be armed and dangerous!"

—*Dr. Dana Gammill*
Cathedral of Life Ministries, Canton, OH

"Sometimes all it takes is a fresh look at a biblical truth. Entering the Decree Dimension revelation was powerful to me personally—especially the understanding that not only will God 'favor' me, but that I will also become 'attractive' to others because of God's glory that comes upon my life! I highly recommend *Daily Decrees for Accessing Abundance* for your library, small group, and congregation!"

—*Stephen Strader*
Senior pastor, Ignited Church
Lakeland, FL

"As I began reading through Joshua's latest book, *Daily Decrees for Accessing Abundance*, I heard this verse of Scripture rise within me: *"Thou shalt also decree a thing, and it shall be established unto thee: and the light shall shine upon thy ways"* (Job 22:28 KJV). Suddenly I knew that this book was going to speak volumes—and it did not disappoint. As you read this book, be ready not only to hear from God, but also to be moved to respond to what you hear, and thereby to experience Him in a fresh, new way! Be blessed and encouraged as I was."

—*Dr. Michael Scantlebury*
Apostle, Dominion-Life International Ministries
Author, *Present Truth Lifestyle*, *Esther: Present Truth Church*, and
Daniel in Babylon

"Absolutely loved this book. It's a timely revelation for the body of Christ. What an honor, what authority, and what changes we can make in the earth as we decree according to His will and His Word. Revelation is wonderful, but Joshua takes it one step further and includes *activation* that will propel us to continue with what we've learned and also help us to create a godly habit. I can hardly wait to start the Daily Decree activations."

—*Dr. Kathy Tolleson*
Kingdom Life Now
Author, *Staying Fresh*

"Joshua Fowler is a great blessing to the body of Christ. I believe his book, *Daily Decrees for Accessing Abundance*, has been released at an opportune time and that it will birth breakthroughs in the lives of believers."

—*Benjamin Ardé*
Founder and president, Arc.tv and Arc Church
Cape Town, South Africa

"As I began to read *Daily Decrees for Accessing Abundance*, I was captivated by the simple yet deep truths that were revealed. This is a must read for every believer—young and old, minister and layman. The pages are filled with prophetic truth established with the precise accuracy of God's written Word. The revelation unlocks knowledge, understanding, and process, allowing anyone to effectively decree and experience spiritual manifestations that will change any situation they are facing. Joshua takes the reader from learning to understanding, and then from understanding to application. This will become one of those books I read over and over."

—*Joe Landreth*
Destiny Development Center, Fort Worth, TX

"A true apostle is marked not only by the battles he's journeyed through, but also by the victories won. When you encounter a man of God who has walked through valleys and mountaintops and yet remains full of hope, in pursuit of life, invested in others, and compassionate, you have found a true gift. Joshua Fowler is marked victorious! We trust his words will encourage and inspire you in your own walk through your valleys and over your mountains. Let the journey begin."

—*Dr. Israel Ashley McGuicken*
Capitol Royal Dynasty

"Nothing happens until someone decrees it! This is starting point of Joshua Fowler's latest book that takes the reader on a journey to discover who they are, why they are alive, and what is available to them. This book is simple yet profound, theological yet practical. It uncovers truth in the Bible and truth in the human heart."

—*Mark W. Pfeifer*
International Director, International Coalition of Apostolic Leaders

"Thank you, Joshua Fowler, for writing *Daily Decrees for Accessing Abundance*. The daily decrees are so powerful that I can't wait until my leadership gets your book and begin walking in abundance!"

—*Bishop Robert E. Joyce*
Rejoyce Ministries

"I have been in the ministry for sixty-four years, but have never read a book that stated so clearly how decrees are to take place. I have spoken decrees in many different circumstances, but have never seen such a comprehensive approach to using them with great effectiveness. The 22-day map of how to use your decrees will not only change your life but will also change your results. I wish I had learned these sixty-four years ago."

—*Apostle Don Lyon DD*
Founder, Faith Center, Rockford, IL

"Joshua Fowler brilliantly lays out the biblical underlying purpose and understanding for decrees and then advances to writing specific decrees. These decrees, declared from a heart of belief, will release powerful, targeted results."

—*Barbara J. Yoder*
Lead apostle, Shekinah, Ann Arbor, MI

"I love the decrees that Joshua provides in his 22-day Decree Challenge. As you align your heart, faith, and mouth with what God is saying, you will see those things come to pass in your life! This book will launch you into a whole new level of seeing God's provision and promises tangibly manifested in your life!"

—*Matt Sorger*
Matt Sorger Ministries

"Joshua Folwer's new book is exceptional and anointed. It will stir you to see your abundance in Christ, and to possess it through decreeing it. I highly recommend it."

—*Dr. Mark R. Van Gundy*
President, Kingdom Legacy Network

DAILY
DECREES
FOR
ACCESSING
ABUNDANCE

DISCOVER THE POWER OF JOB 22

JOSHUA FOWLER

WHITAKER
HOUSE

Daily Decrees for Accessing Abundance:
Discover the Power of Job 22

JoshuaFowler.com
LegacyLife.org
office@joshuafowler.com

ISBN: 978-1-62911-819-2
eBook ISBN: 978-1-62911-820-8
Printed in the United States of America
© 2017 by Joshua Fowler

Whitaker House
1030 Hunt Valley Circle
New Kensington, PA 15068
www.whitakerhouse.com

Library of Congress Cataloging-in-Publication Data (Pending)

1 2 3 4 5 6 7 8 9 10 11 ᴜᴊ 24 23 22 21 20 19 18 17

DEDICATION

I would like to dedicate this book to my oldest son, Hunter, daughter-in-law, Allison, and first granddaughter, Isabella Faith; to my twin daughters, Destiny and Zoë; and to my youngest son, Ben. I am profoundly thankful for your understanding during the many hours I've given to writing this book. I appreciate your commitment to Christ and the ministry He has entrusted to us. I love the way you all fill our home with love, laughter, and worship.

ACKNOWLEDGMENTS

I would like to thank the following people for their encouragement, contributions, and ministry as I've written this book: Mariellen Parks, Zoë Fowler, Destiny Fowler, Charm & Brian Miller, Tyrone & Una McFarland, Jarvis Ovalles, Kirkland & Minerva Allen, David & Suzy Alderman, Angel Noah Dominguez, Tom & Joy Heffner, and Dave Heffner.

My parents, Dr. Charlie & Suzy Fowler, for raising me in an atmosphere of the presence of the Lord and for putting me on the platform to sing and play the drums.

The leaders and members of Legacy Life Church. I'm so blessed to be surrounded by such an awesome team and family.

To my spiritual sons and daughters, both far and near.

To my friends in ministry: Dana and Nan Gammill, Joan Hunter, Patricia King, Mark and Mary VanGundy, Rick and Kay Davison, Michael and Sandra Scantlebury, Tammy Chism, Ryan and Jennifer Deaton, Stephen and Jan Strader, Matt and Stephanie Sorger, Jason and Regina Jones, and J. W. Jones.

CONTENTS

FOREWORD

What we say really does matter. I am mindful of the oft-quoted phrase from the famous late rabbi and theologian Abraham Joshua Heschel: "Words create worlds." His daughter Susannah said this of her father:

> He used to remind us that the Holocaust did not begin with the building of crematoria, and Hitler did not come to power with tanks and guns; it all began with uttering evil words, with defamation, with language and propaganda. Words create worlds, he used to tell me when I was a child, and they must be used very carefully.[1]

Heschel exhibited a mastery of words, both in his writing and in his speaking. When he made the statement, "Words create worlds," it was rooted in the Jewish prayer, "Blessed is God who spoke and the world came into being."

As humans made in the image and likeness of God, it is language that distinguishes us from all the other creatures of the

---

1. Dr. Susannah Heschel, "Abraham Joshua Heschel," http://home.versatel.nl/heschel/Susannah.htm (accessed December 5, 2016).

earth. With language, we are meaning-makers, and we interpret reality. Whatever we say about reality shapes the reality we experience. Words really do matter. The psalmist exercised great wisdom when he prayed, *"Let the words of my mouth and the meditation of my heart be acceptable in Your sight, O LORD, my strength and my Redeemer"* (Psalm 19:14). Words create internal filters of perception, behind our eyes, through which we view the world in front of our eyes. Even one word can shift your perception of reality, faster than the blink of an eye.

When God made humans in His image and likeness and said "Let them rule" (see Genesis 1:26), He was telling them more about who they were rather than what they were to do. They were made vice-regents under His oversight of creation. They were created rulers. The first call to ruler-ship was seen in the power of their words to invoke and evoke destiny in all the beasts of the field and the fowls of the air. Whatever Adam decreed, because of his authority as an image-bearer, was settled. Adam was intended to speak God's decrees after him.

Scripture often speaks of God's righteous decrees and the unrighteous decrees of fallen man. Participating with God in the unfolding of His plan of redemption and restoration involves speaking those things that God has spoken and that He continues to speak, and to speak them with royal authority by the power of the Holy Spirit.

Joshua Fowler has provided a menu of powerful decrees that are derived from the Scriptures, decrees that can help you govern the words that issue from your heart and mouth in a way that will cause you to be fruitful and productive, and will lead you to experience more of the abundant life that Christ has promised for His people. Enjoy the feast he has spread out in each chapter, and more importantly, practice speaking, affirming, and confessing them as you reign and rule in life by Christ Jesus!

—Dr. Mark J. Chironna
Church on the Living Edge
Mark Chironna Ministries
Longwood, FL

1

THE POWER OF THE DECREE

You shall also decide and decree a thing, and it shall be established for you; and the light [of God's favor] shall shine upon your ways. (Job 22:28 AMPC)

THE STORY OF A KING'S DECREE

In centuries past, a king would issue a decree from his throne and that decree would become law throughout all of the provinces and villages of his kingdom. A decree had the force of the law. It was a written document that was very specific in its subject matter and intent. It had to be carried out according to the king's wishes. Failure to obey a decree resulted in severe punishment.

Imagine with me that the king wakes up one morning to discover that the kingdom's crops have yielded an abundant harvest. He makes a decision to issue a decree for all of the citizens to share in the increase of his kingdom by receiving double their allotment of grain.

A few days later, across the kingdom, a distant seacoast village is bustling with the business of everyday life. The local commerce is thriving as people from both far and near haggle and barter in the marketplace just inside the city gates. A little boy chases his sister around their widowed mother's dress as she searches feverishly for one more shekel to purchase enough food to feed her family. A man in danger of losing his farm is trying to sell his horse so he can afford to purchase enough grain to feed his cattle.

From out of nowhere, a man in fine apparel gallops into town through the city gates on a spectacular white horse. He steps down from his mount, clears his throat, and makes a proclamation in a loud voice: "Hear, ye! Hear, ye! The decree of the king!" Around the town square, everyone stops what they are doing and listens intently as the herald declares the king's decree that grain portions are to be doubled. As he finishes a great roar of elation erupts. With one statement, impending doom turns to hope, poverty becomes abundance, and the struggle to survive is converted into the ability to thrive. By the king's decree, law is established and the course of history is changed. The widow and her children who once didn't have enough to eat now leave with their cart full of grain and groceries. The man who almost sold his horse to keep his home, rides home with more than enough grain to feed his livestock.

Although this is a fictional story, throughout history, greater things than this have happened in which the course of lives, nations, and even history were forever changed by a single decree.

One such story is found in the Bible and is actually one of the first recorded decrees in history by a king. In 536 BC, King Cyrus of Babylon issued a decree allowing the Jews to return to Jerusalem to rebuild their temple.

> Now in the first year of Cyrus king of Persia, that the word
> of the LORD by the mouth of Jeremiah might be fulfilled, the
> LORD stirred up the spirit of Cyrus king of Persia, so that he
> **made a proclamation** throughout all his kingdom, and also
> put it in writing, saying,

Thus says Cyrus king of Persia:

All the kingdoms of the earth the Lord God of heaven has given me. And He has commanded me to build Him a house at Jerusalem which is in Judah. Who is among you of all His people? May the Lord his God be with him, and let him go up!   (2 Chronicles 36:22–23)

Think about that! God chose and used a secular king to issue the decree that would free God's people from exile and help them to rebuild the temple of God! Years later, after work on the temple had begun, King Cyrus died and the permission to build the temple was questioned. The issue was brought before the new king, Darius, for a ruling on whether the work could continue.

*Then King Darius **issued a decree**, and a search was made in the archives, where the treasures were stored in Babylon. And at Achmetha, in the palace that is in the province of Media, a scroll was found, and in it a record was written thus:*

*In the first year of King Cyrus, King Cyrus **issued a decree** concerning the house of God at Jerusalem: "Let the house be rebuilt, the place where they offered sacrifices.... Let the expenses be paid from the king's treasury. Also let the gold and silver articles of the house of God, which Nebuchadnezzar took from the temple which is in Jerusalem and brought to Babylon, be restored and taken back to the temple which is in Jerusalem, each to its place; and deposit them in the house of God.... Moreover I issue a decree as to what you shall do for the elders of these Jews, for the building of this house of God: Let the cost be paid at the king's expense from taxes on the region beyond the River; this is to be given* *immediately to these men, so that they are not hindered.*

(Ezra 6:1–3, 4–5, 8)

Not only had the decree freed the Jewish people to return to their home and rebuild their temple, it also paid the construction bill!

In fact, God established a relationship with King Cyrus unlike any other He had with any other non-Jewish king. Here God refers to Cyrus in terms normally reserved for kings of Israel or the Messiah Himself:

> *Thus says the* LORD *to His anointed, to Cyrus, whose right hand I have held—to subdue nations before him and loose the armor of kings, to open before him the double doors, so that the gates will not be shut: "I will go before you and make the crooked places straight; I will break in pieces the gates of bronze and cut the bars of iron. I will give you the treasures of darkness and hidden riches of secret places, that you may know that I, the* LORD, *who call you by your name, am the God of Israel."*   (Isaiah 45:1–3)

According to one Bible commentator:

> God had solemnly set apart Cyrus to perform an important public service in his cause. It does not mean that Cyrus was a man of piety, or a worshipper of the true God, of which there is no certain evidence, but that his appointment as king was owing to the arrangement of God's providence, and that he was to be employed in accomplishing his purposes. The title does not designate holiness of character, but appointment to an office.[2]

---

2. *Notes on the Bible* by Albert Barnes (1834), text courtesy of http://biblehub.com/commentaries/barnes/isaiah/45.htm.

This is a life-changing truth to wrap your mind around. God not only used a secular politician to issue a decree that would free His people and pay for the reconstruction of their temple, but He also established an ongoing relationship with the king by promising to destroy his enemies and make him rich—all so that God's kingdom would expand and bring glory to Him.

This is the power and heritage behind prophetic spiritual decrees. It is not some recent invention by man but a long-established truth recorded in Scripture. For if God was able to use a pagan king to issue decrees that would rebuild temples, defeat enemies, and redistribute vast amounts of wealth, how much more can you and I, as heirs of the kingdom, release decrees that will cause us to access abundance to expand His kingdom and awaken nations for God's glory?

> For you did not receive the spirit of bondage again to fear, but you received the Spirit of adoption by whom we cry out, "Abba, Father." The Spirit Himself bears witness with our spirit that we are children of God, and if children, then heirs—**heirs of God and joint heirs with Christ**, if indeed we suffer with Him, that we may also be glorified together.
>
> (Romans 8:15–17)

A PERSONAL TESTIMONY OF THE DECREE DIMENSION

Recently, I went through an intense and serious legal battle. This battle had the potential of harming and hindering both my family and ministry for many years to come. For a long time, both parties were at a stalemate, legal fees were soaring through the roof, and there seemed to be no end in sight. My attorneys were at a loss for what to do, and so was I. Mediation only made matters worse and it seemed that the more I tried to effect an agreement, the worse things became.

One night, I was invited to a home for worship and prayer. During worship I was overcome with such a sense of hopelessness and despair that I fell on my face and wept uncontrollably. I cried out to the Lord for help. As I continued in worship, the Lord gave me a prophetic word instructing me to minister to a woman across the room. He told me that she should write down a decree and that He would establish it. After I shared this with her and returned to my seat, I heard God say, "Now *you* write a decree, and I will establish it." So I grabbed my iPad and opened an app that allows you to write with your finger. I quickly wrote down my decree regarding the legal matter, then I signed and dated it.

As I was about to leave after service I felt an email register on my phone, so I stopped to read it. Much to my amazement the decree that I had just written down had been established. The other party had agreed to settle and met all of the conditions they had refused to agree to in mediation the day before. It was a miracle!

That night opened my spirit up to the power of a prophetic spiritual decree. As I have studied this, I have discovered that this spiritual dimension that worked for me is open for you, as well. It is greater than any other spiritual dimension I have ever experienced. I've come to know it as the "Decree Dimension." Over the next few chapters, you will discover how to access the abundant inheritance that is rightfully yours as an heir with Christ through living in the Decree Dimension. Then I will invite you to try it on for size during a 22-Day Decree Challenge of faith and miracles.

Are you ready for this? It's time to learn how to enter the Decree Dimension and access the abundant life you have been promised. Here is my decree for you:

I decree that as you read this book and enter into this journey with me, you will never be the same again. You will grow in grace and faith. You will soar on the wings of praise and take your seat with Christ in heavenly places. You will learn how to decree things and they will be established for the glory of God. Other people shall be drawn to you and the brightness of your rising. They will ask you to share with them how you walk in such favor and abundance. You will share about the power of daily decrees and others will learn to live in the Decree Dimension, too! I decree this book will be a catalyst that will raise up a company of believers that will awaken nations and generations for God's glory!

2

ACCESS

Do you like to watch action/adventure movies? So many of the plots include the challenge of gaining access to some secure room or vault. The hero or heroine must overcome one obstacle after another in order to get past the imposing security measures—lasers, guard dogs, armed goons, etc.—in order to access the elusive secrets or treasure hidden inside.

In real life, only people on a pre-approved list can gain access to bank vaults and safety deposit boxes filled with gold, cash, or diamonds. Even so, they still must present the required ID—perhaps a signature, document, fingerprint, or retinal scan. In wealth-laden mansions, family members and staff gain access to secure rooms filled with rare art and priceless valuables by entering a code into a keypad that is known only to them. Treasure-filled safes are protected by a combination known only to the owner. These are among the ways that people protect the things that are most dear to them.

For believers, accessing the treasures of heaven is a somewhat similar process. We must have our ID information in the Lamb's Book of Life in order to gain access to the King of the universe. Then the King gives us the codes to gain access to His treasure, to be used in support of our mission—bringing lost souls to God so He can save them, bless them, and lead them in their divine destiny.

According to the Bible, believers have special access to the throne! Meditate on these verses in Ephesians and Hebrews for a while and see if you can keep from rejoicing and worshiping the Lord.

> *For through [Jesus Christ] we…have access by one Spirit to the Father.* (Ephesians 2:18)

> *But Christ came as High Priest of the good things to come, with the greater and more perfect tabernacle not made with hands, that is, not of this creation. Not with the blood of goats and calves, but with His own blood He entered the Most Holy Place once for all, having obtained eternal redemption.*
> (Hebrews 9:11–12)

> *Seeing then that we have a great High Priest who has passed through the heavens, Jesus the Son of God, let us hold fast our confession. For we do not have a High Priest who cannot sympathize with our weaknesses, but was in all points tempted as we are, yet without sin. Let us therefore come boldly to the throne of grace, that we may obtain mercy and find grace to help in time of need.* (Hebrews 4:14–16)

Spiritual access comes to us when we are born again. It is the most important access we will ever have; everything else we do in our Christian walk is based upon it. Aren't you thankful that the veil has been rent so that you can boldly approach the throne of the Father because of the shed blood of Jesus Christ and the empty tomb? Jesus is our High Priest, who entered into the most holy place in heaven and placed His sinless blood upon the eternal mercy seat, so that we could be a part of God's family forever.

This is why and how we have spiritual access. Now, we can boldly approach our Father God as children!

WHAT IS ACCESS?

Noah Webster's definition of the word "access" in his 1828 dictionary is extremely powerful for what God is doing in the church today.

> Access: Means of approach; liberty to approach; imply-
> ing previous obstacles. By whom also we have *access* by
> faith. Romans 5:2…. Addition; increase by something
> added; as an access of territory.[3]

This definition indicates that spiritual access gives an addition, an increase, and more territory. We are talking about great expansion, being fruitful and multiplying, and taking dominion. There is more to the Christian life than finding peace with God and knowing you'll go to heaven one day after you die. After obtaining access to the Father through Jesus Christ in the spiritual realm, He then gives you access to an addition, an increase, and more territory for His kingdom—all to be used in this life!

> *Every place that the sole of your foot will tread upon I have*
> *given you, as I said to Moses.*   (Joshua 1:3)

> *Enlarge the place of your tent, and let them stretch out the*
> *curtains of your dwellings; do not spare; lengthen your cords,*
> *and strengthen your stakes. For you shall expand to the right*
> *and the left, and your descendants will inherit the nations,*
> *and make the desolate cities inhabited.*   (Isaiah 54:2–3)

---

3. "Access." Webster's Dictionary 1828, Online Edition. *American Dictionary of the English Language.* http://webstersdictionary1828.com/Dictionary/access.

CROSSING OVER

The story of the Promised Land was one of "crossing over." When Moses and the nation of Israel came to Jordan River, they peered over it and into their promised territory. Moses knew his people were tired after the long years of wandering in the wilderness. He did not want to risk a dangerous river crossing without knowing what perils awaited them on the other side. They would not be able to retreat if things got dicey. So Moses dispatched twelve spies to cross over, gather information, and report back.

Ten of the spies returned with bad news:

> Then they told [Moses], and said: "We went to the land where you sent us. It truly flows with milk and honey, and this is its fruit. Nevertheless the people who dwell in the land are strong; the cities are fortified and very large; moreover we saw the descendants of Anak there…. Then Caleb quieted the people before Moses, and said, "Let us go up at once and take possession, for we are well able to overcome it." But the men who had gone up with him said, "We are not able to go up against the people, for they are stronger than we."
>
> (Numbers 13:27–28, 30–31)

The report confirmed that the Promised Land held all the benefits that God had foretold, but it also frightened the people. Only two men were unafraid because they knew that God would not have promised them something that He could not deliver.

> Joshua…and Caleb…, who were among those who had spied out the land, tore their clothes; and they spoke to all the congregation of the children of Israel, saying: "The land we passed through to spy out is an exceedingly good land. If the LORD delights in us, then He will bring us into this land

and give it to us, 'a land which flows with milk and honey.'
Only do not rebel against the LORD, nor fear the people of the
land, for they are our bread; their protection has departed
from them, and the LORD is with us. Do not fear them."

(Numbers 14:6–9)

You've probably heard this story before. God became so angry at the fear and doubt in the Israelites that He made them wait another forty years—until the older generation of Moses died off—before He would lead Joshua and the nation of Israel into their Promised Land. Joshua became their leader because he never doubted the access they had with God. No matter the odds, no matter how big the enemy, Joshua knew they could cross over and enter in because that's what you do when God is ready to work.

It's time for this generation of believers to arise with the same fervor and intensity that was seen in the lives of Joshua and Caleb. God wants you to expand the kingdom of heaven by taking your territories. This is the hour to be a fearless, courageous, holy people who hear the Word of the Lord and are stable in the midst of the storm. But you must be anchored to the Rock—Jesus Christ—so others can turn to you for wisdom and strength when war is raging.

With access to heaven, you can cross over and go where you have not been able to go before. Hearts that have been closed to your testimony of the deliverance of the Lord will now be open. The ears of the people who would not hear your voice before will now be open. They will see Jesus in your eyes. They will hear Jesus in your words. And they will be transformed by God's saving, healing, and delivering power!

God has opened the hearts of the lost to receive Jesus as their Lord and Savior in an unprecedented way—but that is not all!

Although the economy of our nation and the world has been targeted by the enemy, God is now saying, "I'm returning the wealth of the wicked into the hands of the just." (See Proverbs 13:22.) He's doing this so that we can expand His kingdom in the earth.

VISITATION

I want to tell you about a spiritual vision I had in 1998. In the vision, Jesus came into my room and stood at the foot of my bed. He said, "Your name shall be Joshua." He lifted me up and out of that room, and I went with Him through the ceiling and into another world. I was in a body of water that was like liquid gold, flowing up under my neck like waves. Then Jesus spoke again, saying, "Your name shall be Joshua. Lead My people into their promised land."

He told me that I would be an apostolic and prophetic demonstration in the earth of a twenty-first-century Joshua, and that I would be a sign to the body of Christ that it is time to leave Egypt and cross over into our promised land. His words were like water pouring out of His mouth and into my belly. The vision seemed as though it went on forever but in reality it was only for a short time. When I "came to myself" I was shaking. The next morning when I awoke, my name was changed. My inner being was changed. I stumbled out of bed and into the kitchen, still shaking. To this day I'm still coming into a natural understanding of the message He poured into my spirit almost two decades ago.

About a year and a half prior to that day, while I was preaching on Elisha's double portion of blessing (see 2 Kings 2:1–13), the Holy Spirit released a prophetic word through me: "Your wife will conceive and she'll give birth in 1998, and it will be a sign of my harvest in the earth."

On September 8, 1998, God blessed us with our twin daughters, Destiny and Zoë. For me, they represent the harvest of souls coming forth in the earth.

A MODERN-DAY ADVENTURE

I'm telling you this because I believe that God has commissioned me as a "Joshua" to help you cross over to access your promised land and reap the greatest harvest of souls of all time. I submit to you that one of the primary access codes to obtain God's treasure is making daily decrees according to His Word. As we issue God's decrees, things are set in motion, the windows of heaven burst open wide, and supernatural blessings and favor begin flowing into our lives. As we decree, doors will fly open, the anointing of the Holy Spirit will pour through us, and we will access the supernatural resources we need to reap the greatest harvest of souls this world has ever known.

Are there things that you've been praying for, things God has promised and you've been waiting to see come to pass? Well, it is time for access! What was promised to you, even years ago, will come to pass. It's time to receive what you've been crying, hoping, and praying for. It is not the time to merely dream and talk about your destiny, it's time to decree it and see it manifest! In the coming pages we will explore together how to access abundance for the expansion of the kingdom of God.

3

ACCESSING ABUNDANCE

And with great power the apostles gave witness to the resurrection of the Lord Jesus. And great grace was upon them all. Nor was there anyone among them who lacked.

(Acts 4:33–34)

WHY WE MUST ACCESS ABUNDANCE

It takes money to do the things that God has called you to do. There's no way around it. God is our Provider, the All-Sufficient One, and money is the commodity He uses in the earth to get things done. Money itself is not evil; it is *"the love of money"* (1 Timothy 6:10) that is evil.

Believers must break out of their poverty-riddled, just-get-by mentalities if the church is going to win the world to Jesus. Maybe in the past you've said, "All those prosperity preachers are just out to get my money. I can't stand to listen to them."

Would you rather listen to poor preachers?

Don't you want God's prosperity and blessings?

Don't you want to understand God's financial system?

If that is how you think, then I have one more question for you: How can you reach the nations of the world if you can barely pay your own bills?

WHAT CONSTITUTES ABUNDANCE?

When you hear the word *abundance*, most likely the first thing you think of is *finances*. But there is so much more to abundance than just finances. Abundance comes with our access to the Father. It is the indwelling of the Holy Spirit and God's Word.

> *Blessed be the God and Father of our Lord Jesus Christ, who has blessed us with **every spiritual blessing** in the heavenly places in Christ.*   (Ephesians 1:3)

Abundance in the natural realm comes from abundance in the spiritual realm. When we are born again, we receive *"every spiritual blessing,"* and without them, we will never obtain natural blessings. That's why the eyes of our understanding need to be enlightened.

> *That the God of our Lord Jesus Christ, the Father of glory, may give to you the spirit of wisdom and revelation in the knowledge of Him, the eyes of your understanding being enlightened; that you may know what is the hope of His calling, what are the riches of the glory of His inheritance in the saints.*   (Ephesians 1:17–18)

We must draw close to the Father to receive wisdom and revelation so that we can see and know the true riches. Aren't you thankful for just one word from God's throne? When we study the first chapter of Ephesians, we are stunned by the simple truth about abundance. God is our treasure, and we are His treasure. Our riches are found in Him, and His riches are found in us and in all the souls we win to His kingdom.

> *Then you shall see and become radiant, and your heart shall swell with joy; because the abundance of the sea shall be turned to you, the wealth of the Gentiles shall come to you.*   (Isaiah 60:5)

VISION OF AIRCRAFT CARRIER

This verse in Isaiah speaks of *"the abundance of the sea."* The sea represents lost humanity. In the vision, I was suspended above a sea with Jesus. In the sea were millions of bobbing heads, which He told me represented the sea of lost humanity. There were several tugboats in the sea that represented ministries. Jesus asked, "Why won't they come together?"

"I don't know," I replied.

Jesus said these ministries were building man-made kingdoms; they were not extending His kingdom. Then James 5:16 rolled across the horizon: *"Confess your trespasses to one another, and pray for one another, that you may be healed. The effective, fervent prayer of a righteous man avails much."*

Jesus said to me, "If they would only come together and confess their faults, they would be healed."

He dipped His hand beneath the sea and began pulling the plugs. One by one, the tugboats began to sink. Many of the people who were on board those ministries sank beneath the sea of lost humanity, and others were barely holding on to floating bits from the capsized tugboats.

Then the fog rolled away. I saw an aircraft carrier with five planes on its deck. Jesus explained that this Spirit-filled aircraft carrier was His ministry, and He was giving stewardship over it to me and several others. He told me that the planes represented the five-fold ministries. He told me to study them, because I was called to bring them together.

Jesus told me that the control tower represented divine order and government, which He was bringing back to His church. As we stood and watched, several planes landed and took off. When a plane would land, those aboard the aircraft carrier would rejoice at the testimonies of the successful missions. Then they would refuel the planes with the Word, prayer, and resources before launching them again. There were also rescue helicopters that would land on the deck, loaded with those they had rescued out of the treacherous waters of sin.

In the years that have passed since that day, God has continued to give me and our ministry team more insight and understanding concerning the Spirit-filled aircraft carrier and our mandate to raise up and send out people who will awaken nations and generations for Christ.

THE *SOLE* PURPOSE IS THE *SOUL* PURPOSE!

The *sole* purpose is the *soul* purpose. When you rise up as a soul-winner, as a reaper, you'll begin to see financial abundance flow into your life, which will allow you to reap an even greater harvest. There is such a harvest coming to the church right now!

If you want to access the abundance of God's blessings, then you've got to stop thinking about yourself, your own needs, and your own situation. Begin reaching out to other people who have needs. If you want access, acceleration, and abundance, go out and reap the harvest of souls that is waiting to hear the good news.

You're not going to see the financial harvest God has promised until you are primarily concerned about the soul harvest. You have to be kingdom-minded. When you get kingdom-minded about the souls of the earth, you're going to begin to see your destiny released and *"all these things shall be added to you"* (Matthew 6:33).

*But you be watchful in all things, **endure afflictions, do the work of an evangelist**, fulfill your ministry.*

(2 Timothy 4:5)

You say, "Well, I'm not called to be an evangelist." The Bible doesn't say you have to be called to be an evangelist. It just says to *"do the work of an evangelist."* You cannot establish full proof of your ministry without doing the work of an evangelist.

I also want you to notice that winning the lost and making full proof of your ministry requires you to *"endure afflictions."* It's hard to read the book of Acts and not recognize that sobering truth, and yet many believers still miss it. By their insistence on staying within their comfort zones and not growing up, they remain blind to the lost who are passing by them every day. There are mile markers of growth in both the natural and spiritual life, and they usually have to do with relinquishing old habits, crucifying the flesh, and coming to a new level of selflessness.

A vivid example of this is when our twin daughters, Destiny and Zoë, were three years old and we had a pacifier throwing-away party. We prepared the girls for months in advance by telling them that the day was coming when we were going to throw away their "binkies." We got them real excited. While we were at the lake one day, we saw a turtle, so I said, "We're gonna give that turtle your pacifiers. And that turtle's babies are gonna love your pacifiers."

Zoë and Destiny agreed, saying, "We're gonna be big girls. We're gonna throw away our 'pacies'!" So we took them down to the water and they threw their pacifiers in the lake. We rejoiced. We clapped our hands. We had a big time because now they were big girls.

When it was time for bed that night, Destiny went right to sleep. But Zoë decided she was going to throw a fit. And this fit went on for a long time! The next night it went on for a long time again. As Zoë sobbed, "I don't want to be a big girl. I don't want to be three. I want to be this many. I want to be two. I don't want to grow up!" I remember thinking, *My God, how am I going to sleep if this girl doesn't have her pacifier?*

Zoë, of course, was not so different from many Christians today who struggle with spiritual growth. When pastors challenge their people to grow up in God, they begin to scream and cry in protest. Out of frustration, a lot of pastors put binkies back in people's mouths to keep the peace. There are believers who have been sitting in the pews for forty years or more, still sucking on their pacifiers! They are there every Sunday and Wednesday, Jesus is their Lord and Savior, and they're going to heaven, end of story—and end of growth.

The hallmark of spiritual growth is measured in how we love God, how we love one another, and how we care for the lost. But to do that, we have to give up our pacifiers. We have to *"endure afflictions"* and *"do the work of an evangelist"* in order to make full proof of our ministry.

ABUNDANCE IN YOUR ABUNDANCE

If believers would just go win souls and apply God's Word, none of our members would lack for anything within the next few years. They would have a book-of-Acts experience:

> And with great power the apostles gave witness to the resurrection of the Lord Jesus. And great grace was upon them all. Nor was there anyone among them who lacked.
>
> (Acts 4:33–34)

For example, let's say God gives you a great business idea but you don't have the finances to act on it. Instead of sitting at your desk all day, racking your brain on how to get finances, you go out to win people at your job to Jesus. Perhaps some of them decide to join your church. After a while they experience spiritual growth.

One day, one of them thinks, *Man, I don't want to finance things that are ungodly anymore.* They look around the church and ask themselves, *Who has a godly business idea? Let me invest in that.* Just like that, you have received what you needed to bring your lucrative business idea to fruition!

The Bible is a practical book. This is not something that's "out there." You win somebody to the Lord, then, after a while, they begin to help you win others and fulfill your destiny. Soon the world begins to change. It's biblical multiplication that suggests "one can put a thousand to flight, but two can put ten thousand to flight." (See Deuteronomy 32:30.) First, you must care about what God cares about. Then access, acceleration, and abundance will come pouring into your life.

ARISE, SHINE!

Arise, shine; for your light has come! And the glory of the LORD is risen upon you. For behold, the darkness shall cover the earth, and deep darkness the people; but the LORD will arise over you, and His glory will be seen upon you. The Gentiles shall come to your light, and kings to the brightness of your rising. (Isaiah 60:1–3)

There has to be a rising up in order for there to be a harvest of souls. In order for God to arise upon you, you must rise and shine. There has to be a step of faith on your part. You and I must rise to the occasion. And once we rise and shine, we'll begin to see the lost, kings, and nations drawn to the brightness of our rising, who is Jesus Christ.

You will arise and have mercy on Zion; for the time to favor her, yes, the set time, has come. (Psalm 102:13)

Kairos is an ancient Greek word meaning the right or opportune moment. I've been preaching about the *kairos* moment for years, but recently the Holy Spirit has begun to connect the dots. I'm beginning to see the picture more clearly now. Our moment of accessing abundance comes when we get busy with the Father's business. When you rise and shine, your set time will come. Your due season will come.

Have you forgotten about *your* harvest of souls? I'm talking about *your* sphere of influence, the people under *your* ministry. These are the sheep in your pasture. Even if you are waiting to start your own ministry or have your own pulpit, you should be faithfully ministering to the people on your job, in your family, and in your neighborhood. These people are out of the reach of the most successful TV pastor and the greatest missional evangelist. But you see them every day because God has put you there. Love those who are not loved, provide for those who need something, and I prophesy to you that you are going to come into your set time, your *kairos* moment.

> You are the salt of the earth; but if the salt loses its flavor, how shall it be seasoned? It is then good for nothing but to be thrown out and trampled underfoot by men. You are the light of the world. A city that is set on a hill cannot be hidden. Nor do they light a lamp and put it under a basket, but on a lampstand, and it gives light to all who are in the house. Let your light so shine before men, that they may see your good works and glorify your Father in heaven.
>
> (Matthew 5:13–16)

God didn't save you and write your name in the Lamb's Book of Life so you could sit at home and watch Christian television. He didn't fill you with the Holy Spirit and give you His Word just for you to stand up and say, "I'm filled with the sweet Holy Spirit, and I love God's Word," and then sit back down. He saved you, filled you with the Holy Spirit, and gave you His Word so that you could be a witness for Him.

> But you shall receive power when the Holy Spirit has come upon you; and you shall be witnesses to Me in Jerusalem, and in all Judea and Samaria, and to the end of the earth. (Acts 1:8)

Where is your Jerusalem? If you're not faithful over your Jerusalem, then you're never going to see "the end of the earth." If you want to impact the nations, then impact your block and your workplace. Arise, shine! Abundance comes to people who rise to the occasion and serve where God positions them.

Look around. Who is lost? Who on your job needs prophetic direction? Who needs healing? Who needs food, clothing, or shelter? Wouldn't you love to be so prosperous that you could go down your block, find out who is having trouble financially, and pay all of their bills for them? Wouldn't you love to pay off the mortgage of every member of your family? Think big! God does.

If you see somebody who is confused, why not go home and fast and pray about it? You should say, "God, they don't know what they're doing. They have confusion in their lives. And God, I know that if You will use me as a vessel to minister to them, they will believe that You are the Lord who saves. Give me direction and wisdom. Give me prophetic insight. Let me go to them and prophesy Your word to them, because I know they will come to You."

But no, all too often, we only want the gifts of the Spirit to operate in *church*—and usually for our own benefit! We go to the altar, get our little prophesies, write them down, and then we go home to pray about it. Then we wonder why nothing else happened. Prophetic ministry is not merely so we might get a word from God, write it down, and pray over it. That is good and necessary, but it is only the beginning.

The Bible says in Proverbs 11:30, *"He who wins souls is wise."* That was written by Solomon, who, besides Jesus Christ, was the wisest man who ever lived. His kingdom was greater than his father David's. The glory of Solomon's temple was so awesome that when the Queen of Sheba came to visit, she fainted. (See 2 Chronicles 9:1–12.) You want increase? Reap your harvest!

The gifts of the Spirit are to operate through us when we go out to reap the harvest. We are to prophesy over people who are lost so they can come into the kingdom of God. If you want a prophetic word, then you need to sow a prophetic word. You reap what you sow.

People come to me and ask, "Why don't you ever prophesy over me?"

I say, "Maybe you're not prophesying over anybody else."

How many people do you see in a week, but you fail to tell them about the goodness of God? How many people do you see in a week, but you don't even care for their souls? If you'll start thinking about them as the harvest of God, you'll reap that harvest.

4

KEYS FOR ABUNDANCE

And I will give you the keys of the kingdom of heaven, and whatever you bind on earth will be bound in heaven, and whatever you loose on earth will be loosed in heaven.

(Matthew 16:19)

EP 5:17
6:11

True biblical prosperity is not about you or me or what we can obtain. It's about expanding the kingdom of God and reaping the harvest of souls.

Have you ever asked yourself why so many people seem unable to possess their God-given promises? Have you grown tired of religious reruns and merry-go-round ministries? Are you asking questions like the elderly lady in the old Wendy's commercial, "Where's the beef?"

WHERE'S THE HARVEST?

Where are the signs and wonders, miracles and healings?
Why are there so many empty seats in churches today?
Where's the breakthrough?

If these are the questions you have been asking, then you are among the company of many believers who, like myself, have a holy dissatisfaction for wasting time wandering aimlessly in the wilderness.

Child of God, you are called to possess! You have not come to the kingdom to be a Wilderness-Walker. You have been chosen to cross over, enter in, and possess the land! You are called to be a Promise-Possessor! How can we arise and possess the land? How will the church enter into the reaping anointing to gather the greatest harvest of all time?

REBUILDING THE TABERNACLE

According to the Word of God, when we become a part of rebuilding the tabernacle of David, we position ourselves for possession. Let's take a look at what that means.

"On that day I will raise up the tabernacle of David, which has fallen down, and repair its damages; I will raise up its ruins, and rebuild it as in the days of old; that they may possess the remnant of Edom, and all the Gentiles who are called by My name," says the LORD who does this thing.

(Amos 9:11–12)

After this I will return and will rebuild the tabernacle of David,…so that the rest of mankind may seek the LORD.

(Acts 15:16–17)

Perhaps you are asking yourself, *Is this is really for today? And if so, how we can participate in this rebuilding?* Yes, it is for today. Starting with King David and his son Solomon, this pattern has been handed down as an eternal, heavenly pattern.

Then David gave his son Solomon the plans for the vestibule, its houses, its treasuries, its upper chambers, its inner chambers, and the place of the mercy seat; and the plans for all that he had by the Spirit, of the courts of the house of the LORD, of all the chambers all around, of the treasuries of the house of God, and of the treasuries for the dedicated

> *things.… "All this," said David, "the* LORD *made me under-*
> *stand in writing, by His hand upon me, all the works of these*
> *plans."*   (1 Chronicles 28:11–12, 19)

Every leader who followed the pattern that David received from the Lord possessed promises and prospered. The Word of God gives accounts of seven leaders who followed this pattern of the tabernacle of David. Nehemiah rebuilt the walls by building as David did. (See Nehemiah 11–12.) Hezekiah fortified the walls to ward off invading enemies. (See 2 Chronicles 32.) Isaiah, and later Jesus, called the tabernacle of David a *"house of prayer"* in Isaiah 56:7 and Matthew 21:13. The apostle John revealed the beauty of the tabernacle of David in Revelation 4 and 5.

In Acts 13:2, we see the priestly principle of ministering to God as found in the tabernacle of David. In this passage, leaders ministered to God and, as a result, the apostles Paul and Barnabas were sent forth to change the world. We find that once the tabernacle of David was rebuilt, God's glory overtook cities and nations. As this happens in the church today, we will reap the greatest harvest of souls that this world has ever known.

REBUILDING OUR TABERNACLE

The only way to rebuild the tabernacle of David is to create a habitation in which God can dwell. We do so through *intense, corporate praise and worship* and through *united, fervent intercessory prayer.* This requires pure, sincere hearts in the men and women who will set their eyes on the Lord.

> *Go and tell My servant David, "Thus says the* LORD: *'Would you build a house for Me to dwell in?'"*
>   (2 Samuel 7:5)

The desire of God's heart remains the same today: "Build Me a house. Establish a place for Me to inhabit." We do this through intentionally building a habitation of worship. When we worship, we are building a dwelling place for the Lord, putting out the welcome mat and pulling out a seat for Him to sit on.

WHAT WILL WE POSSESS?

"Behold, the days are coming," says the LORD, *"when **the plowman shall overtake the reaper**, and the treader of grapes him who sows seed; **the mountains shall drip with sweet wine**, and all the hills shall flow with it. I will bring back the captives of My people Israel; **they shall build the waste cities** and inhabit them; **they shall plant vineyards and drink wine from them; they shall also make gardens and eat fruit from them**. I will plant them in their land, and **no longer shall they be pulled up from the land** I have given them," says the Lord your God.*

(Amos 9:13–15)

Here are just five of the many blessings we can receive when we position ourselves to possess by rebuilding the tabernacle of David.

+ We will *possess* the harvest (souls, souls, and more souls).
+ *We* will *possess* new wine (refreshment, renewal, and revival).
+ *We* will *possess*, rebuild, and inhabit cities (urban transformation).
+ We will *possess* provision (and the devil won't be able to steal it).
+ We will *possess* the land (forever, never to be evicted).

WAGING WAR AND RELEASING WEALTH

Judah also will fight at Jerusalem. And the wealth of all the
surrounding nations shall be gathered together: gold, silver,
and apparel in great abundance.   (Zechariah 14:14)

"Judah" means "praise," so this verse tells us that praise also
has the ability to fight. I'm talking about "battle-cry praise." Some
of you may not be aware that there is more to praise and worship
than just singing hymns and choruses on Sunday morning. Lifting
our praises to God is not only an obedient expression of our love
and awe for Him, it is also a powerful tool of spiritual warfare.
Those who dare to enter into their promised land soon discover
that there are forces who aren't just going to let you saunter in
and take over. The enemy isn't going to give up territory without a
fight. Eventually, you will come to the place in which it seems you
are outgunned and outmanned.

Many know the story of Jericho, the first city in the Promised
Land that had to be taken. The Israelites marched around that
city playing instruments and praising God and the walls of the
city fell. (See Joshua 6:1–27.) But a lesser known story of praise on
the battlefield is when King Jehoshaphat came against a coalition
of Ammonites and Moabites. Jehoshaphat knew the odds were
against him. It is in such times, when the forces aligned against
you seem overwhelming, when the battle must be carried out in
the spiritual realm. King Jehoshaphat prayed:

*Now, here are the people of Ammon, Moab, and Mount
Seir—whom You would not let Israel invade when they
came out of the land of Egypt, but they turned from them
and did not destroy them—here they are, rewarding us by
coming to throw us out of Your possession which You have*

given us to inherit. O our God, will You not judge them? For we have no power against this great multitude that is coming against us; nor do we know what to do, but our eyes are upon You.   (2 Chronicles 20:10–12)

In this moment of desperation, God raised up a prophetic voice—Jahaziel. Not really one of the more famous names in the Bible, is it? But Jahaziel boldly prophesied to the nation of Israel:

Listen, all you of Judah and you inhabitants of Jerusalem, and you, King Jehoshaphat! Thus says the Lord *to you: "Do not be afraid nor dismayed because of this great multitude, for the battle is not yours, but God's. Tomorrow go down against them…. You will not need to fight in this battle. Position yourselves, stand still and see the salvation of the* Lord, *who is with you, O Judah and Jerusalem!" Do not fear or be dismayed; tomorrow go out against them, for the* Lord *is with you.*   (verses 15–17)

Armed with the promises of God, the Israelites marched into battle.

Jehoshaphat stood and said, "Hear me, O Judah and you inhabitants of Jerusalem: Believe in the Lord *your God, and you shall be established; believe His prophets, and you shall prosper." And when he had consulted with the people,* **he appointed those who should sing to the** Lord, **and who should praise the beauty of holiness, as they went out before the army** *and were saying: "Praise the* Lord, *for His mercy endures forever." Now* **when they began to sing and to praise, the** Lord **set ambushes against the people of Ammon, Moab, and Mount Seir, who had come against Judah; and they were defeated….** *When Jehoshaphat and his people came to take away their spoil, they found among* *them an abundance of valuables on the dead bodies, and precious jewelry, which they stripped off for themselves, more than they could carry away; and they were three days gathering the spoil because there was so much.* (verses 20–22, 25)

Praise wages spiritual warfare and releases wealth. Maybe you only lift your hands in praise when you get something. It's great to praise and thank God when you get something but what if you need something? If you need something, lift your hands up and give Jesus praise. If you'll give Him praise then, you'll see your enemies flee and your God arise.

Let God arise, let His enemies be scattered; let those also who hate Him flee before Him.   (Psalm 68:1)

HOW DOES GOD ARISE?

God arises through the praises of His people. When we lift Him up, He rises in our midst and puts our enemies to flight. He sets an ambush for our enemies. We need to get into the mindset that praise is not just something we do at church. Praise Him at home. Dance around your living room. Magnify God in your house, in your car, wherever you go. Why? Because your praise fights. And then, harkening back to Zechariah 14:14, *"the wealth of all the surrounding nations shall be gathered together: gold, silver, and apparel in great abundance."*

Are you ready to possess the harvest? Are you thirsty for the new wine of the Holy Spirit? Would you like to be a part of transforming your city? Does living in the land of more than enough sound good? Are you tired of being a Wilderness-Walker? If so, trade in your sandals for mountain boots and arise as a Promise-Possessor today. Let's arise as King Jehoshaphat did when he received the word of the Lord. Let's arise with a Davidic anointing as Nehemiah and Hezekiah did, wielding the sword of praise with one hand and the trowel of prayer with the other hand. Together we will rebuild the walls of the tabernacle of David and possess the land!

IT'S ALL ABOUT GOD AND HIS HOUSE

> *Now for the house of my God I have prepared with all my might: gold for things to be made of gold, silver for things of silver, bronze for things of bronze, iron for things of iron, wood for things of wood, onyx stones, stones to be set, glistening stones of various colors, all kinds of precious stones, and marble slabs in abundance. Moreover, **because I have set my affection on the house of my God**, I have given to the house of my God, over and above all that I have prepared for the holy house, **my own special treasure of gold and silver**.*
>
> (1 Chronicles 29:2–3)

"Because I have set my affection on the house of my God," what will happen? I have "*my own special treasure of gold and silver.*"

Abundance comes when you put God's house first, when your affection is toward the house of God. When you take care of God's house, He takes care of your house. Your love and concern should be toward your house of faith, your family of believers.

If you show up every Sunday and sit there, saying, "Amen! Praise God, and glory be to Jesus," that does not release the increase into your hands. But throughout the week, if you're lifting up the leaders and the congregation in prayer, if you're taking part and serving in the activities of the church, then God will release wealth and increase to you.

So you haven't done it yet? Repent, and old things are passed away, behold all things become new! There is no condemnation if you are in Christ Jesus, but you've got to walk not after the flesh but after the Spirit. (See Romans 8:1.) Determine right now to set your affection on the house of God. You'll have your own *"special treasure,"* and that's called *abundance.*

Abundance is moving from "just getting by" into "overflowing." Our God is not known for just getting by. He's *El Shaddai,* which means "God Almighty," the God of more than enough. But He is looking to see where your heart is. Is it with Him and the house He's placed you in? The kingdom of God is within you and me, and we can see His kingdom extended by becoming a part of a local family of believers.

A PERFECT HEART

> *Then the people rejoiced, for they had offered willingly, because with a loyal heart they had offered willingly to the Lord; and King David also rejoiced greatly.*
>
> (1 Chronicles 29:9)

I think it's really interesting that the Holy Spirit describes a perfect heart in terms of giving to the Lord—for a building project! The people were helping David see his dream of building the temple of the Lord come true. The people gave willingly toward that building project and rejoiced in their giving. As a result, when the temple was built and Solomon became king, Israel saw the greatest time of abundance and peace it had ever known.

A perfect heart loves the house of the Lord and His people.

A perfect heart brings forth abundance.

BLESSED TO BE A BLESSING

> *Now the Lord had said to Abram: "Get out of your country, from your family and from your father's house, to a land that*

I will show you. I will make you a great nation; I will bless you and make your name great; and you shall be a bless-
ing."   (Genesis 12:1–2)

If you live your life always searching for a blessing, a miracle, or a breakthrough, then how are you going to bless anybody else? God wants to bless you so that when you show up, you are a blessing to others. Every time you come into a room, people should sense the presence of God, and if there's a financial need, you should be able to reach into your pocket and meet it.

ORDAINED TO BE A BLESSING

When we say we want to bless nations, I'm not just talking about staging a little puppet show or renting a building for two hundred people and using a karaoke machine with a mic for preaching. I'm talking about going there and putting on a concert bigger than any rock band could put on. I'm talking about sending an entire church to a nation to shake it with the power of God.

How do we do that?

We must be blessed to be a blessing. There have to be resources released to us.

For whoever has, to him more will be given, and he will have
abundance; but whoever does not have, even what he has will
be taken away from him.   (Matthew 13:12)

God's kingdom does not operate as a welfare system. There are no handouts and there is no victim mentality. In God's financial system, you have to be proactive and aggressive—a producer. You must use what you have.

Look at the parable of the talents in Matthew 25:14–30. The master gave three of his servants talents and then left them. When he returned, the first two servants had doubled their talents, but

the third servant, afraid that he would lose his, buried
master was furious with the third servant, took his talen
him, and gave it to the first servant.

A person who is blessed to be a blessing is a person who
reproduces and multiplies what God has given them. They don't
hoard it for themselves. They don't tremble with worry and fear
that they won't have enough. They put their faith in God and
get out there and multiply so that they can be a greater blessing
and win more souls for the kingdom.

THE TRUTH ABOUT THE "PROSPERITY MESSAGE"

There are two gutters on either side of God's truth about
prosperity, and each one is able to totally mess up your personal
relationship with the Lord. One gutter, or extreme, is the belief
that you can automatically have whatever you confess. You can get
that Cadillac. You can have that house. You can receive that yacht.
You just confess it and possess it, name it and claim it. You can have
anything and everything. People caught in this extreme-thinking
gutter become materialistic, greedy, self-centered, and selfish.
This gutter is filled with arrogance and pride. But the worst part
is that it reduces God to a formulated slot machine. Just put in
your confession and out comes whatever you're "believing God
for." There's no relationship. Instead of seeking Him and finding
out what He has for your life, *you* decide what your life should be
and what you should have. In the end, you wind up seeking *things*
instead of seeking *Him*. Eventually, when you name it and claim it
and you don't get it (or you get it but it messes up your life), you get
mad at God. This gutter perverts your relationship with God by
making Him into a benefactor instead of a Father.

The other gutter is much more subtle but equally devastating. It is the belief that to be a pure-hearted, humble Christian, you must be poor and not want for anything. You live your life affecting no one except those you bump into—infecting them with the lie that being poor equates with being holy. That is a lie and, like materialism, it also leads to arrogance and pride. It is thinking, *Oh, those terrible rich folk think they know God, but they will never know the holiness I'm walking in with holes in my shoes and my leaky roof.*

What you don't realize is that those "terrible rich folks" are the ones who have the resources to take Jesus to the world! Their money sends missionaries around the world, builds centers to feed the hungry and clothe the naked, and opens medical clinics in remote and impoverished areas. Those "terrible rich folks" are often the vital support lines for ministries that are bringing Jesus to the lost and dying—and come to your rescue when you can't feed your family!

This gutter, again, is subtle. You're not humbling yourself before God; you're humbling yourself in the eyes of your brothers and sisters. You're trying to make your church believe you're humble when actually you're just ignorant of God's Word and living below your ability to be blessed and be a blessing. You have put the spotlight on yourself and your "humility" instead of on God and His provision. This gutter perverts your relationship with God by making Him into a stingy miser instead of a loving, generous Father.

> *And you shall remember the Lord your God, for it is He who gives you power to get wealth, that He may establish His covenant which He swore to your fathers, as it is this day.*   (Deuteronomy 8:18)

Here's an access verse. God gives you the ability and supernatural power to get wealth. Why? So you can establish His covenant in the earth. In New Testament terms, that means you don't want things; you want Him. You don't want to show off your riches; you want to show off Him. You don't want people to see a benefactor; you want them to see Jesus.

You want to be so blessed that you can take off two weeks a year and go with the missions team to impact nations. You want to be so blessed that you can feed the hungry. You want to be so blessed that you're not worried about paying for your own kid's shoes; in fact, you can pay for the shoes of other people's kids. When you get that in perspective, then you can be blessed to be a blessing—and that is true humility. You're just a vessel being used by God to get His blessings to others.

WHO DOES GOD BLESS?

Once again, the Bible doesn't say that money is evil, it says that *"the love of money"* is the root of all evil. That's when your possessions possess you instead of God possessing your possessions. If you are willing to give away everything you have, then the things you have don't possess you. If you own anything right now that you're not willing to give up for the gospel, then it owns you. No man can serve two masters. You either serve God or mammon. (See Matthew 6:24.)

God blesses those who can handle what He gives to them. Remember, *need* does not move God; *faith* moves God. When you arise in faith, take what God puts in your hand and multiply it, give Him the glory and honor with it, and use it to be a blessing to His kingdom, then God can give you even more. That's what the master did for his servants who multiplied their talents.

*His lord said to him, "Well done, good and faithful servant;
you were faithful over a few things, I will make you ruler
over many things. Enter into the joy of your lord."*

(Matthew 25:21)

We're not about trying to get things; we're about seeking the
King of Kings. We seek Him first and His righteousness, and
these other things are added to us. (See Matthew 6:33.) We don't
go around naming it and claiming it, blabbing it and grabbing it, or
touching everything and saying, "It's mine." No, we simply believe
that God will provide everything we need to accomplish the call
He's given us to reach the world.

We take what God puts in our hands, we use it to advance
His kingdom, we recognize the *sole* purpose is the *soul* purpose,
and we confess with our mouths that Jesus is Lord and that He
must be lifted up. When we lift Him up, guess what happens? All
men are drawn to Him. (See John 12:32.)

The finances that have been held up are released in abundance, because God says, "I've given them something and they're
not hoarding it. I've given them My Son and they're not hoarding
Him. They're giving Him away."

"We have this treasure in earthen vessels" (2 Corinthians 4:7).
You have a treasure inside of you right now! You have *"Christ in
you, the hope of glory"* (Colossians 1:27). Do not shut up your
wells of compassion and walk by people who don't know Jesus.
Go to them, give them the love of Jesus, reach out and touch
them, hug them, embrace them, tell them that He loves them.
Then watch and see if what has been held back from you is suddenly released.

*Blessed are those who hunger and thirst for righteousness, for
they shall be filled.*

(Matthew 5:6)

Hungry folks get blessed. Lazy and apathetic folks do without.

DOUBLE FOR YOUR TROUBLE

Are you experiencing trouble? You're in good company. Most of the generals of the faith, such as David, Moses, Joshua, Peter, and Paul, all experienced trouble. Release the decree and you will see that God will give you double for your trouble.

Let that settle into your spirit a moment. You've paid a price to see your family, your city, and your nation won to the Lord. If you will endure and battle until you see victory, you will not only win your personal battle, but you will win a double harvest of souls.

In Luke 4, Jesus warred in the wilderness armed only with God's Word. When He emerged from the wilderness, what is the first thing He did? He opened the scroll of Isaiah and read it in the synagogue. Most Bible historians say that He most likely read this whole passage, not just the few verses that are recorded in Luke 4:

The Spirit of the Lord God is upon Me, because the Lord has anointed Me to preach good tidings to the poor; He has sent Me to heal the brokenhearted, to proclaim liberty to the captives, and the opening of the prison to those who are bound; to proclaim the acceptable year of the Lord, and the day of vengeance of our God; to comfort all who mourn, to console those who mourn in Zion, to give them beauty for ashes, the oil of joy for mourning, the garment of praise for the spirit of heaviness; that they may be called trees of righteousness, the planting of the Lord, that He may be glorified. And they shall rebuild the old ruins, they shall raise up the former desolations, and they shall repair the ruined cities, the desolations of many generations. *Strangers shall stand and feed your flocks, and the sons of the foreigner shall be your plowmen and your vinedressers. But you shall be named the priests of the* LORD, *they shall call you the servants of our God. You shall eat the riches of the Gentiles, and in their glory you shall boast.* **Instead of your shame you shall have double honor,** *and instead of confusion they shall rejoice in their portion.* **Therefore in their land they shall possess double;** *everlasting joy shall be theirs.*

(Isaiah 61:1–7)

According to Isaiah, you are given a double portion for your shame, a portion of the spoils of war for your confusion, and double the territory! Isaiah 61:7 says, *"Instead of your shame you shall have double honor, and instead of confusion they shall rejoice in their portion."* What you reap will be far greater than what you sow. You will access abundance like never before as you issue heavenly decrees.

5

WHAT'S SO SPECIAL ABOUT YOU?

By this point you may be thinking, *I get that God is awesome. I get that spiritual decrees and prophecies are real. I get all that, but I'm a nobody. I've never been to seminary. I'm no pastor or prophet or apostle. Why should I think that I'm so important that God is going to listen and react to a decree issued from little ol' me?*

Part of entering into the Decree Dimension is understanding who God is, but just as important is understanding who you are. You are not just some foot soldier in the army. You are not a cowering servant begging for crumbs. According to Scripture you are the rightful heir of the kingdom and all that entails.

Let's return to Romans 8:

For as many as are led by the Spirit of God, these are sons of God. For you did not receive the spirit of bondage again to fear, but **you received the Spirit of adoption** *by whom we cry out, "Abba, Father." The Spirit Himself bears witness with our spirit that* **we are children of God, and if children, then heirs—heirs of God and joint heirs with Christ,** *if indeed we suffer with Him, that we may also be glorified together.* (Romans 8:14–17)

And then to Galatians 3:

> *For you are all sons of God through faith in Christ Jesus.*
> *For as many of you as were baptized into Christ have put*
> *on Christ. There is neither Jew nor Greek, there is neither*
> *slave nor free, there is neither male nor female; for you are*
> *all one in Christ Jesus. And if you are Christ's, then you are*
> *Abraham's seed, and* **heirs according to the promise**.
>
> (Galatians 3:26–29)

You are not just a member of a religion, one among millions. You are family. You have been adopted in, written into the will, and a full participant in the family inheritance. Let that sink in.

Just as in life, inheritance is not based on what you do; it's based on who you are. There's nothing you can do to receive an inheritance. You just have to be born into, or adopted by, the family.

INHERITANCE VERSUS HARVEST

Don't confuse inheritance with harvest. Harvest is something you work for. It is something you must sow in order to reap. Inheritance is only because of who you are. You are an heir. Harvest is something you must wait for. You do not have to wait for inheritance like you wait for harvest; you just walk in it. You simply have to be who God has called you to be, and mature into who God has designed you to be—then your inheritance is released. Just as in real life, inheritance is released upon maturation. If you remain a child, you won't be able to walk in the privileges that are rightfully yours. But even in immaturity, you are still an heir.

> *Now I say that the heir, as long as he is a child, does not differ*
> *at all from a slave, though he is master of all, but is under*
> *guardians and stewards until the time appointed by the*
> *father. Even so we, when we were children, were in bondage*

*under the elements of the world. But when the fullness of the time had come, God sent forth His Son, born of a woman, born under the law, to redeem those who were under the law, **that we might receive the adoption as sons**. And because you are sons, God has sent forth the Spirit of His Son into your hearts, crying out, "Abba, Father!" Therefore you are no longer a slave but a son, and if a son, then an heir of God through Christ.* (Galatians 4:1–7)

Being sons (and daughters) gives you rights and access that comes with being an heir. Part of your inheritance is nations and generations. Part of your inheritance is financial security, prosperity, and living in "more than enough." It's really very simple: If you don't have, how can you give to impact nations? If all you're ever doing is scrounging for enough money to pay your own bills, how can you ever make an impact on nations and generations?

There are people who never receive their inheritance because they never knew they were named in someone else's will. They are completely unaware that they are heirs and that their money is being held up in court. So it is in the Spirit. A lot of people never enter into inheritance because they don't realize that it's already theirs. You have an inheritance of signs and wonders and miracles. You think that miracles only happen when Benny Hinn comes to town, but the Bible says, *"these signs will follow those who believe"* (Mark 16:17). You may be pining for the days of Kathryn Kuhlman's healing ministry and not recognize that there is a greater One that is inside of you that can flow through you right now. It's all included in your inheritance.

"For you are all sons of God through faith in Christ Jesus. For as many of you as were baptized into Christ have put on Christ" (Galatians 3:26–27). You don't need decades of Bible school or

anointed people to blow on you. You are in Christ! You have put Him on as a new garment. You are an heir. Now, when you stand before someone who is demon-possessed, they don't see you. They see Christ, the Heir of the Father, who conquered death, hell, and the grave. When you stand before someone who is demon-possessed, you stand clothed in Christ and you speak, or decree, as Christ. When you see sickness, you don't stand as someone pleading, "Oh, Jesus, please do this for me." No, you recognize that you are an heir of the kingdom. Healing is your portion. When you stand before someone who is sick and extend your hand, the King Himself is extending His hand to release healing.

Think of England. Think of the royal princes and princesses. Cameras follow them and record their every move. Why? Because they have royal blood. They walk in the power and authority of royalty. What they say and do matters. Likewise, the enemies of our souls are looking at us to see what we are going to do. The world is waiting, the earth is groaning, all in anticipation of you rising up as a rightful heir. Wherever you walk has been claimed for the King.

You have the authority—anointing—to rise up in heavenly places and pass sentence on the enemy's words and plans. I'm not just talking about the office of pastors or prophets or apostles. This is for anyone who believes. This is for you and me. It's great to get agreement in prayer from those in leadership. But sometimes, you don't have time to find an apostle. Benny Hinn might not be on TV right now. Sometimes a believer needs to rise up in his or her own authority and declare truth. "The prayers of the righteous avail much." (See James 5:16.) They work.

Here is a secret for you: the earth does not belong to the devil. It's ours. Our Father bought it back when He sent Jesus. It's all part of our inheritance.

*May the LORD give you increase more and more, you and
your children. May you be blessed by the LORD, who made
heaven and earth. The heaven, even the heavens, are the
LORD's; **but the earth He has given to the children of
men.*** (Psalm 115:14–16)

*Ask of Me, and I will give You the nations for Your inheri-
tance, and the ends of the earth for Your possession.*
(Psalm 2:8)

WHY DO WE INHERIT ALL THIS?

Our vision must line up with our inheritance. We are not
making all of this up. It's not the latest fad or a whim. It is biblical,
based on God's Word.

*Now therefore, in the sight of all Israel, the assembly of the
LORD, and in the hearing of our God, be careful to seek out
all the commandments of the LORD your God, that you may
possess this good land, and **leave it as an inheritance for
your children after you forever.*** (1 Chronicles 28:8)

God has included you as heir of the promises He gave to
Abraham. He wants you to possess this land and leave it for an
inheritance for your children after you—forever.

*Joshua took the whole land, according to all that the LORD
had said to Moses; and Joshua gave it as an inheritance to
Israel according to their divisions by their tribes. Then the
land rested from war.* (Joshua 11:23)

We receive our inheritance in order to divide and distribute it.
We are part of the ongoing promise to Abraham that his descendants
would bless nations. We have been adopted into that promise. God
wants to bless you so that you can be a blessing. Your inheritance is

not just for you. It's for you to distribute and give away, through the works of your hands and feet and the decrees of your mouth.

H-E-I-R

Here is an acrostic to help you remember what it means to be an heir who issues prophetic decrees according to God's will.

H–Heritage

Whatever the enemy tries to bring against you in life, you have the power as an heir—a heritage—to say, "no weapon ever formed against me will prosper!" (See Isaiah 54:17.) That doesn't mean a weapon won't be formed or brought against you. But when it is, you have the heritage to rebuke it in the name of the Lord. When something comes against your health, finances, or career, you can knock it down.

We are part of a family line and our Father desires that we rule and reign with Him.

> *Who is the man that fears the Lord? Him shall He teach in the way He chooses. He himself shall dwell in prosperity, and his descendants shall inherit the earth.* (Psalm 25:12–13)

> *I traverse the way of righteousness, in the midst of the paths of justice, that I may cause those who love me to inherit wealth, that I may fill their treasuries.* (Proverbs 8:20–21)

This is our family heritage. We are not meant to struggle in poverty, living paycheck to paycheck. We are to prosper so that we may pass that prosperity on to others.

E–Empowered

We are empowered to prosper, overcome, and succeed.

*So [Jesus] got into a boat, crossed over, and came to His own city. Then behold, they brought to Him a paralytic lying on a bed. When Jesus saw their faith, He said to the paralytic, "Son, be of good cheer; your sins are forgiven you." And at once some of the scribes said within themselves, "This Man blasphemes!" But Jesus, knowing their thoughts, said, "Why do you think evil in your hearts? For which is easier, to say, 'Your sins are forgiven you,' or to say, 'Arise and walk'? But that you may know that the Son of Man has power on earth to forgive sins"—then He said to the paralytic, "Arise, take up your bed, and go to your house." And he arose and departed to his house. Now when the multitudes saw it, **they marveled and glorified God, who had given such power to men.*** (Matthew 9:1–8)

This is the same Jesus who lives inside of you. The same Jesus who healed and walked on water is living inside of you. You have power over sickness and disease. You have power over anything the enemy sends your way.

Now to Him who is able to do exceedingly abundantly above all that we ask or think, according to the power that works in us. (Ephesians 3:20)

The same creative power that said, *"Let there be light..."* (Genesis 1:3) is inside of you. Why do you need to be empowered? Because there are things in life you will face that you cannot overcome without this power. How are we empowered?

I-Infilling of the Holy Spirit

The Holy Spirit is the seal of our inheritance.

In Him also we have obtained an inheritance, being predestined according to the purpose of Him who works all things

according to the counsel of His will, that we who first trusted
in Christ should be to the praise of His glory. In Him you
also trusted, after you heard the word of truth, the gospel
of your salvation; in whom also, having believed, **you were**
sealed with the Holy Spirit of promise, who is the guaran-
tee of our inheritance *until the redemption of the purchased*
possession, to the praise of His glory. (Ephesians 1:11–14)

When you receive the infilling of the Holy Spirit, you receive
the guarantee that the rest is yet to come. God is putting a down
payment on your life. It's His earnest money. When you receive
the Holy Spirit, you become a witness. Why does He want you to
be a witness? Why does He want you to be an heir that receives
an inheritance? So that you can establish His covenant on the
earth.

If you really want to move into what God's Word says—the
provision, the favor, the power, the increase, the divine health and
wholeness—then it is imperative that You receive the infilling of
the Holy Spirit. It's already been paid for. Christ didn't receive the
stripes upon His back so that you could live in poverty and sickness. He did it so you could live the abundant life now!

But He was wounded for our transgressions, He was bruised
for our iniquities; the chastisement for our peace was upon
Him, and by His stripes we are healed.   (Isaiah 53:5)

If you are hungry, you will be filled. The problem is, some
people just aren't hungry enough. When it comes to church, "a
little dab will do ya." They're fine with a few songs, some shout-
ing, and a sermon, but they don't want it to affect the rest of their
lives.

When you get filled with the Holy Spirit, you aren't your own
anymore. You don't have Him; He has you.

R–Revelation

When you are filled with the Holy Spirit, you receive a revelation of Christ and who you are in Him.

Simon Peter answered and said, "You are the Christ, the Son of the living God." Jesus answered and said to him, "Blessed are you, Simon Bar-Jonah, for flesh and blood has not revealed this to you, but My Father who is in heaven. And I also say to you that you are Peter, and on this rock I will build My church, and the gates of Hades shall not prevail against it. (Matthew 16:16–18)

As soon as Peter properly identified the Lord, he received his own identity. His name changed and he visualized his destiny. When you identify Christ—when you receive Him as your Savior—and you get a revelation of who He is in your life, you will begin to discover who you are and your destiny on the earth. You'll find your purpose, the reason you were put here. It wasn't just to take up space for seventy years. It's to make a difference and leave a legacy that changes nations and generations.

CHRIST IN YOU

The main thing you need to understand is that when the enemy sees you, he sees Christ Jesus. Christ's blood brought us into a place in which we could access our inheritance.

In order for you to receive an inheritance, someone needs to leave a will and testament, and then they have to die. Similarly, Jesus came and cut a new covenant with His people. He fulfilled the old covenant and established a new covenant. But in order for that new covenant to be ratified, it had to be sealed with blood. In the old covenant, it took the blood of rams and goats and bulls. But in the new covenant, it was the spotless Lamb.

> *Let this mind be in you which was also in Christ Jesus, who, being in the form of God, did not consider it robbery to be equal with God, but made Himself of no reputation, taking the form of a bondservant, and coming in the likeness of men. And being found in appearance as a man, He humbled Himself and became obedient to the point of death, even the death of the cross.*   (Philippians 2:5–8)

When His blood fell to the earth the covenant was ratified. When He died they laid Him in a tomb, but He rose then on the third day, triumphant over death, hell, and the grave, and now sits at the right hand of the Father, advocating on our behalf and making sure that we get what is rightfully ours in the covenant that He established for us.

> *And if you are Christ's, then you are Abraham's seed, and* **heirs according to the promise**.   (Galatians 3:29)

Our promise is "as far as the eye can see." (See Genesis 13:15.) Our promise is multiplication.

In the coming pages you will discover the Decree Dimension. I believe the truth you are about to receive will totally revolutionize your prayer life and faith walk. Just as the Lord told Joshua in Joshua 3, you've not been this way before. Open your heart and follow closely asking the Holy Spirit to reveal His truths regarding decrees.

6

THE DECREE DIMENSION

*Thou shalt also **decree** a thing, and it shall be established
unto thee: and the light shall shine upon thy ways.*
(Job 22:28 KJV)

*You will also decide and **decree** a thing, and it shall be established for you; and the light [of God's favor] shall shine upon
your ways.* (Job 22:28 AMPC)

God wants you, as His change agent here on earth, to begin to
see that you have the ability to make decisions and decrees that
will alter the course of history. You are a history-maker. You are
a world-changer. You are an earth-shaper. You are an heir of the
King! God put you here for such a time as this. Your words matter.
What you say and do has the power of life and death in it. If you
decree a thing, *"it shall be established."*

The dictionary defines the noun *decree* as "an official order
given by a person with power or by a government…having the
force of law." As a verb, it is defined as "to order or decide (something) in an official way…to command or enjoin…to determine or
order judicially."

The first mention of *decree* in Scripture is found in the above verse. The Hebrew word translated as "*decree*" is *gazar*, which means "to cut, divide, cut in two, snatch…destroy, exterminate."[4]

In context, exegetically speaking, a decree ushers in God's formal and authoritative order from the highest court of the third heaven into our natural realm. Decrees carry the force of law and command and ordain things to shift and manifest. These decrees are judicial decisions and orders that are irreversible. Decrees cut through circumstances, divide darkness, split mountains, and destroy obstacles to serve an unredeemable sentence on the defeated foes of darkness.

When you decree God's Word, you are bringing things into alignment with the will of the King. I'm talking about a dimension that many believers have never entered into. Most believers live out their lives of faith in the realm of *petition*. The "Petition Dimension" is okay, but God wants His children to move into the Decree Dimension, where we are no longer just petitioning God for something to happen, but instead we are sitting with Him in heavenly places and issuing the divine decrees. In the Decree Dimension your prayers change. You no longer say, "O Lord, would you help me? I need you to help me, God. O Jesus, please! O God, please help me with my finances." Instead, you now decree, "Send now prosperity!"

> *"Save now, I pray, O Lord; O Lord, I pray, send now prosperity."* (Psalm 118:25)

This is a whole other dimension. You have the authority, according to God's Word, to decree, "*on earth as it is in heaven*" (Matthew 6:10) and see it manifest right where you are!

---

4. "H1504—*gazar—Strong's Hebrew Lexicon (NKJV)." Blue Letter Bible.* Accessed 19 Oct, 2016. https://www.blueletterbible.org/lang/lexicon/lexicon.cfm?Strongs=H1504&t=NKJV.

DECREES ARE LIKE ARROWS

Like arrows in the hand of a warrior, so are the children of one's youth. Happy is the man who has his quiver full of them.   (Psalm 127:4–5)

...your descendants shall possess the gate of their enemies.
(Genesis 22:17)

Let's look at these Scriptures in 3D.

First, see yourself as an arrow and decree. Second, see your seed/children, both natural and spiritual, as arrows/decrees. Third, see your words as arrows/decrees. You are a decree sent from God. You are a living epistle. When you know you have been sent as an arrow of decree to hit the mark, your very presence will make a statement and shift atmospheres as you go. Both your natural and spiritual children are arrows of decree that will possess the gates of cities. Your words are decrees, and when properly aligned with God's Word, they will be established.

An arrow has three components: the shaft is the long portion, straight and balanced; the arrowhead is weighted and sharp for trajectory and piercing; the fletching, or the feathers, give it spin and balance, accurately moving it to its target. When an archer pulls back the bow, he or she wants to make sure that the arrow has a straight shaft, that it is upright.

Just as it takes time for an arrow to become straight, it takes time in your life to properly align with God's Word.

Don't be like some who say, "I'm already an arrow and I'm ready to hit the mark now!" Remain humble and teachable so that if God wants to balance or sharpen you, He can. The fletching, or feathers, on the back of an arrow helps it to spin more accurately toward the target. So, once you are sharp and straight, continue to be open and teachable so new things can be added to your life, then you will be more accurate in the Spirit. As one of God's arrows, you will hit the mark. Allow this process to take place in all three dimensions. Embrace it as an arrow into your personal life. Embrace it for future generations, both naturally and spiritually. We can always become sharper arrows and more skillful archers so that the words/decrees we release will make the impact they are intended to make.

But remember to heed the process, even if it humbles. Just as David's five smooth stones had to go through a smoothing process in water before he used them to defeat Goliath, we also must go through a similar process so that we can hit the mark. Sometimes God will use our leaders or other believers to smooth out our rough edges. If you embrace the process and resist running from it, you will become as effective as David's stone. God will use you to take out giants in your spheres of influence.

STAY SHARP

Listen, O coastlands, to Me, and take heed, you peoples from afar! The LORD has called Me from the womb; from the matrix of My mother He has made mention of My name. And He has made My mouth like a sharp sword; in the shadow of His hand He has hidden Me, and made Me a polished shaft; in His quiver He has hidden Me. And He said to Me, "You are My servant, O Israel, in whom I will be glorified." (Isaiah 49:1–3)

God wants to make your mouth so sharp that when you release decrees, just like Samuel, not one word will fall to the ground. He wants to make your mouth sharp so that every decree will hit the mark. He said, *"My word...shall not return to Me void, but it shall accomplish what I please, and it shall prosper in the thing for which I sent it"* (Isaiah 55:11). He wants to make your mouth a sharp sword. He wants to make you a polished shaft. He wants to hide you in the quiver of His house so that when it's time, He can pull you out, draw you back, and send you to take the gates of the enemy. You will open your mouth, draw back that bow, and issue decrees of heaven. He wants you to see that your words, when aligned with heaven, are weapons that will penetrate.

And He raised us up together with Him and made us sit down together [giving us joint seating with Him] in the heavenly sphere [by virtue of our being] in Christ Jesus (the Messiah, the Anointed One). (Ephesians 2:6 AMPC)

According to Ephesians 2:6: *"God...raised us up together, and made us sit together in the heavenly places in Christ Jesus."* That means that Jesus is at the right hand of the Father, and you are right next to Jesus. That means you can look down upon your circumstances and adversaries from your seat in the "*heavenly sphere.*" You can look down and laugh upon the enemies of the cross.

> *The kings of the earth set themselves, and the rulers take coun-*
> *sel together, against the LORD and against His Anointed....*
> *He who sits in the heavens shall laugh; the LORD shall hold*
> *them in derision.*   (Psalm 2:2, 4)

According to Psalm 2, I'm sitting with Him and my enemies are dashed to pieces.

> *Ask of Me, and I will give You the nations for Your inher-*
> *itance, and the ends of the earth for Your possession. You*
> *shall break them with a rod of iron; You shall dash them to*
> *pieces like a potter's vessel.*   (verses 8–9)

Now, as one sitting at the right hand of the Lord as he sits at the right hand of the father, I look down, I draw back my bow, and I begin sending decrees forth. I decree *this* shall happen; I decree *this* comes to an end; I decree *this* shall now be established and shall be in order—all according to Scripture.

This is the power of Job 22. You need only to agree with God's Word by deciding and decreeing. Let's remind ourselves of God's Job 22 promise:

> *You shall also **decide** and **decree** a thing, and it shall be*
> *established for you; and the light [of God's favor] shall shine*
> *upon your ways.*   (Job 22:28 AMPC)

Decide and decree that poverty is stricken from your family lineage starting now. Decide and decree that you are the head and not the tail. You shall lend and shall not borrow. Decide and decree over your family that sickness and disease is moved far from your home, starting right now with this generation. Diabetes comes to a halt starting right now with this generation. Cancer comes to a halt. Decide and decree that you are healed by His stripes. And none of these things shall come near you or your house. God says, in effect, "Come up and sit with Me and you will surely see what you decree. You are kings and priests. I've put a signet ring on your hand and whatever you bind on earth is bound in heaven, and whatever you loose on earth is loosed in heaven. You just have to decide and decree it."

I will declare the decree of the Lord…. (Psalm 2:7 AMPC)

If I decree it, it's established. If I decree it, I will see it. I have to send something in order to see something. What goes up must come down. The rains of your tomorrow are the decrees of your today. If He's going to do anything in the earth He's going to do it through you and me. We have legal right and authority to decree a thing and see it established. Get God's word on your lips, draw back the bow of your mouth, and launch arrows of decrees.

In Luke 4, when Jesus faced temptation in the wilderness He answered by saying, *"It is written…."* He was using the written Word of God to release decrees to vanquish His enemy—Satan. So don't just memorize Scripture—decree it!

Before you ask, decide and decree. We have spent too much time pleading and making petitions. We need to move into the Decree Dimension!

THE DECREE OF THE WATCHERS

This decision is by the decree of the watchers.

(Daniel 4:17)

The prayer of a person living right with God is something powerful to be reckoned with. (James 5:16 MSG)

Take heed, watch and pray…. (Mark 13:33)

...praying always with all prayer and supplication in the Spirit, being watchful to this end with all perseverance and supplication for all the saints....   (Ephesians 6:18)

I have set watchmen on your walls, O Jerusalem; they shall never hold their peace day or night. You who make mention of the LORD, do not keep silent, and give Him no rest till He establishes and till He makes Jerusalem a praise in the earth.   (Isaiah 62:6–7)

God is raising up a company of watchers all over the world. These watchers will not hold their peace, day or night, and are releasing decrees on behalf of the destiny of churches, cities, nations, and generations. This company will watch and pray from the Decree Dimension, ushering in awakening and abundance, the likes of which have never been seen before. Are you one of them? If so, take your post, release the decrees, and get ready to receive a harvest.

7

TEN KEYS FOR DECREES

1. DECIDE IT. DO IT.

Commit and start today with Day 1 of the 22-Day Decree Challenge. Begin your life in the Decree Dimension now! Don't just sit there; get up and do it! If you want to experience the power of the decree, stay the course and continue to do it for the next twenty-two days. Why twenty-two days? Well, it's been said that it takes twenty-one days to make or break a habit. Daniel fasted and prayed for twenty-one days. And you are probably thinking, *Joshua, can you count? That's twenty-one!* And you would be right, but now is the time to go to the next dimension. It's time to go beyond where you've been. In praying about this Daily Decree Challenge, I felt in my spirit that there is a correlation between the number of decrees and Job 22:28—thus, the 22-Day Decree Challenge! It's my desire and belief that this will not end on Day 22, but that it will become your new lifestyle—issuing decrees that will awaken nations and generations for Christ!

2. TARGET IT. READ IT.

What is the purpose of the decree? What outcome is desired? Once your "target" is identified, search for God's Word regarding the matter. Remember, it's not your mind over the matter; it's God's Word over the matter. Don't just come up with stuff on your own and then try to force it into a Scripture verse that sort of agrees with it. A decree is simply God's Word at work in your situation, applied to your life, and claimed by your tongue. Fill yourself with God's Word and then release decrees from the overflow of your spirit, which is in communion with Him.

> *So then faith comes by hearing, and hearing by the word of God.* (Romans 10:17)

> *Be diligent to present yourself approved to God, a worker who does not need to be ashamed, rightly dividing the word of truth.* (2 Timothy 2:15)

> *By the word of the LORD the heavens were made, and all the host of them by the breath of His mouth.* (Psalm 33:6)

> *By faith we understand that the worlds were framed by the word of God, so that the things which are seen were not made of things which are visible.* (Hebrews 11:3)

> *For the word of God is living and powerful, and sharper than any two-edged sword, piercing even to the division of soul and spirit, and of joints and marrow, and is a discerner of the thoughts and intents of the heart.* (Hebrews 4:12)

> *Your word is a lamp to my feet and a light to my path.* (Psalm 119:105)

3. WRITE IT. SIGN IT.

Once you get God's Word on the matter, write it down or type it out. Now that you're armed with the truth of His Word, write a few sentences or paragraphs based on what you've received.

What's the primary thing required on an official document? A signature. So now that you've written the decree, make sure you sign it to make it official. You might ask, "How does my signature make it official?" Because you're a King's kid. You are an heir and joint heir with Christ Jesus. When you sign the decree, you're saying, "I'm coming into agreement with the Word of God and I'm not coming out of agreement. I will agree with the decree until I see it come into reality."

> Then the LORD answered me and said: "Write the vision
> and make it plain on tablets, that he may run who reads it.
> For the vision is yet for an appointed time; but at the end it
> will speak, and it will not lie. Though it tarries, wait for it;
> because it will surely come, it will not tarry."
>
> (Habakkuk 2:2–3)

4. DATE IT.

Once you've decreed it, make sure to write down the date. Often times, unless you date an official document, it's not official. Although heaven records everything, it is powerful to look back and see how far God has brought you. I'm so thankful there were people such as Ezra, Luke, and others who took the time to give details such as dates and times when the Lord did certain things. By documenting the dates and timelines of your decrees, it will serve as a testimony of God's faithfulness for you, your children, and your children's children. Generations to come will be able to read of God fulfilling His Word as you decreed it.

5. DECREE IT.

Take the decree you've written and issue it. Declare it aloud! Send the decrees as arrows into the atmosphere. There's something about hearing a word from the Lord. You need to hear the decree. Let the decree roll off your tongue and into your heart. Let the decree come into your eye's gate. Release it from your mouth's gate. Let it come into your ear's gate and make its way into your heart's gate. As you do the word will come alive, and the decrees will go forth and begin to demonstrate the will of the King in the gates of the city and wherever you've sent them.

I will declare the decree of the Lord.... (Psalm 2:7 AMPC)

You shall also decide and decree a thing, and it shall be established for you; and the light [of God's favor] shall shine upon your ways. (Job 22:28 AMPC)

6. POST IT. GUARD IT.

Now that you've issued the decree, post it so that you, and those in relationship with you, can see it and agree with it. Post it on your doors, your refrigerator, and your bathroom mirror. Post it on the visor of your car, on your computer screensaver, the wallpaper on your cellphone. Facebook it, Instagram it, Tweet it, and pin it on Pinterest. Post it anywhere and everywhere God puts on your heart so that you keep it before your eyes and before those who know you.

Some might ask, "What if it doesn't happen?"—to which I respond, "What happens when it does?" Put a sentry to guard your mind and your mouth against negativity and unbelief going in or out. How are you going to act when you see the decree come to pass? Get ready, because it *will* come to pass. Why do others need to see the decree? So they will know the power of God that is working in and through your life, so they might be awakened to a life in Christ, and so that other believers will move into deeper realms of the Decree Dimension.

And you shall write them on the doorposts of your house and on your gates, that your days and the days of your children may be multiplied in the land of which the LORD swore to your fathers to give them, like the days of the heavens above the earth. (Deuteronomy 11:20–21)

…casting down arguments and every high thing that exalts itself against the knowledge of God, bringing every thought into captivity to the obedience of Christ….

(2 Corinthians 10:5)

7. DECLARE IT. SEE IT.

Continue to declare it at least twice daily—when you awaken and before going to sleep. Be determined and persistent. See it through the eyes of faith until you see it manifested in the natural realm.

And the LORD said to Abram…: "Lift your eyes now and look from the place where you are—northward, southward, eastward, and westward; for all the land which you see I give to you and your descendants forever. (Genesis 13:14–15)

Moreover the word of the LORD came to me, saying, "Jeremiah, what do you see?" And I said, "I see a branch of an almond tree." Then the LORD said to me, "You have seen well, for I am ready to perform My word."

(Jeremiah 1:11–12)

Like Abraham, lift your eyes and see all that God has for you. As with Jeremiah, keep watching for God is going to accelerate the fulfillment of His Word. When you see it by faith, it will come to pass!

For we walk by faith, not by sight. (2 Corinthians 5:7)

While we do not look at the things which are seen, but at the things which are not seen. For the things which are seen are temporary, but the things which are not seen are eternal.

(2 Corinthians 4:18)

8. RECEIVE IT. RECORD IT.

Now that you have decreed it, receive it by faith. Praise Him and begin to act as if it has already happened! Just as a receiver on a football team has to run the route before he can catch the ball, God is throwing touchdown passes—breakthrough and abundance to those who will run and receive it! Don't just sit there and say, "Send it down!" Use your faith. Come into alignment with heaven. Get into position and you'll receive what you have decreed. Record the date when you receive the promise.

Therefore I say to you, whatever things you ask when you pray, believe that you receive them, and you will have them.

(Mark 11:24)

But let him ask in faith, with no doubting, for he who doubts is like a wave of the sea driven and tossed by the wind. For let not that man suppose that he will receive anything from the Lord; he is a double-minded man, unstable in all his ways.

(James 1:6–8)

9. SHARE IT.

Don't keep it to yourself! Now that you know the power of the Decree Dimension, go and share it with others. Become a part of the Decree Company and testify to others what God is doing in your life. Share with them how easy it is to move into this higher dimension with Christ. Freely you have received, freely give it to others. Just think of what will happen in your church when others learn to decree! Just think what can happen in your school or on your job! Imagine what can happen in your neighborhood and your city when an army of archers arise, releasing arrows of decrees! Destinies will be realized; lives will be changed; financial breakthroughs will occur; revival and awakening will ignite; miracles, signs, and wonders will manifest; and a great harvest of souls will be reaped. Absolutely anything can happen!

Heal the sick, cleanse the lepers, raise the dead, cast out demons. Freely you have received, freely give.

(Matthew 10:8)

You are the light of the world. A city that is set on a hill cannot be hidden. Nor do they light a lamp and put it under a basket, but on a lampstand, and it gives light to all who are in the house. Let your light so shine before men, that they may see your good works and glorify your Father in heaven.

(Matthew 5:14–16)

10. REFLECT ON IT. REPEAT IT.

Apply what you've learned right now! Join me in this 22-Day Decree Challenge and release the first of twenty-two decrees for accessing abundance! As each decree is fulfilled, reflect and correct. Were you consistent and did you persist in standing firm against any opposition? Was your aim steady and true as you launched the arrow of decree at the target? Repeat the steps for all twenty-two decrees and then write your own decree on Day 23. What is the next mountain that needs to come down, the next personal need that is looming, the next enemy encampment that requires intervention? Each time you repeat the process, your faith muscles will grow stronger.

Are you ready? Sign and date the commitment statement that follows and you will be ready to enter the Decree Dimension!

22-DAY DECREE CHALLENGE

I, _Teresa DeMatos_, take the 22-Day Decree Challenge and will read it, write it, sign it, date it, decree it, post it, see it, receive it, share it, and do it. I will do it with passion daily believing God for His Word to be fulfilled in my life, family, church, city, and world.

Signature: _Teresa DeMatos_

Date: _May 30, 2018_

DAY 1

THE DECISION DECREE

You shall also decide and decree a thing, and it shall be established for you; and the light [of God's favor] shall shine upon your ways. (Job 22:28 AMPC)

You'll decide what you want and it will happen; your life will be bathed in light. (Job 22:28 MSG)

Starting today, I decree the decree, make the decision, and decide what the outcome will be by the way I act and the words I speak. The power of death and life are in my tongue, for by it I decide what will be done.

I won't live in fear but I will live by God's Word and decrees. Away with delays and poverty that were spawned by apathy and indecision, for now is my season of supernatural favor and provision.

Supporting Scriptures: Proverbs 18:21; 2 Timothy 1:7; Luke 4:4; Psalm 102:13

Signature: _Tusa DeMater_

Decree Date: _May 30, 248_

Additional Decree Details:

_____

_____

_____

_____

Daily Decree Notes:

Today I decided to post these decrees, because I am not ashamed of God or His Word! If people don't like it, they can unfriend me. I am accepted in the beloved!

Date the Decree Was Received: May 30, 2018

Decree Testimony:

The fear of posting is gone!

_____

_____

_____

_____

_____

DAY 2

THE BLESSING DECREE

Blessed be the God and Father of our Lord Jesus Christ, who has blessed us with every spiritual blessing in the heavenly places in Christ. (Ephesians 1:3)

I decree that God's Word trumps every other word concerning my life and financial wellbeing. Let every man be a liar for God's Word is true.

I am the head and not the tail; I am above only and never beneath. I lend and don't have to borrow. I'm blessed coming and going; blessed in the city and blessed in the field.

My children and their children's children are blessed and lack for no good thing. I am blessed in my body. I am blessed in my finances. I am blessed in my relationships. I am blessed in my family. I am blessed in every area of my life.

I am blessed, blessed, blessed, blessed—blessed to be a blessing.

Supporting Scriptures: Romans 3:4; Deuteronomy 28:13; Proverbs 10:22; Genesis 28:13–15; Psalm 66

Signature: _Trisa DeMater_

Decree Date: _5-31-18_

Additional Decree Details:

The word for today in my daily reading is

_____

_____

_____

Daily Decree Notes:

_____

_____

_____

_____

Date the Decree Was Received: June 3, 2018

Decree Testimony:

- Lee hit a deer riding his motorcycle to New Hampshire. He hit the head of it & it's body slammed into his leg, but he did not fall, the bike stayed straight - Blessed in His coming & going - He is the head! not the tail - Never beneath only above! Thank you Jesus!! Glory to You only!

DAY 3

THE ABUNDANCE DECREE

And God is able to make all grace (every favor and earthly blessing) come to you in abundance, so that you may always and under all circumstances and whatever the need be self-sufficient [possessing enough to require no aid or support and furnished in abundance for every good work and charitable donation]. (2 Corinthians 9:8 AMPC)

I decree I am a lender and not a borrower. I have favor in whatever I do and I'm blessed in every area of my life! Wells of wealth are in my homes. Thank You, God, for all the blessing You have promised me. I decree every word that God has spoken over me regarding prosperity will come to pass as His holy written Word.

I decree that I am "Abraham rich," blessed with an abundance of God's favor, dispensing good to others, and not lacking in any good thing. I receive the wealth of the nations, peace, prosperity, and wholeness in every area of my life, in Jesus' name.

Supporting Scriptures: Ephesians 3:20; 3 John 2; Philippians 4:19; Psalm 23:5; John 10:10; Proverbs 3:10

Signature: _Tirsa DeMator_

Decree Date: _June 1, 2018_

Additional Decree Details:

I'm my daily reading the Psalm 119: 153-
154 - Argue my case, take my side - Protect
my life as You promised. The wicked are from
rescue, for they do not bother w/ your decrees!

Daily Decree Notes:

Psa. 119: 171 - Let Praise Flow from my
lips, for you have taught me your
decrees.

Date the Decree Was Received: June 1, 2018

Decree Testimony:
Right After decreeing - this
a woman from our church came to our
door - excited because she got a
check in the mail that was unexpected.
The amount was $55.00 which represents
(grace, grace) - double portion!

DAY 4

THE ROYAL DECREE

But you are a chosen generation, a royal priesthood, a holy nation, His own special people, that you may proclaim the praises of Him who called you out of darkness into His marvelous light. (1 Peter 2:9)

I decree the Word of the Lord over my life and over everything that I set my hands to.

I declare that as a priest of the Lord, I am a chosen race, a royal priesthood, a holy nation, a people who are God's own possession. God has made me so that I may speak of the wonderful acts of the One who has called me out of darkness into His amazing light.

Therefore, I decree the word of the Lord with full assurance, knowing that this Word that has gone out of Your mouth shall not return to You void. It will never be useless and non-productive, but it shall accomplish that which You have destined and purposed. It shall prosper in the thing which You have sent and assigned it to.

Supporting Scriptures: Psalm 134:3; Daniel 9:18–22; John 17:19; Philippians 1:6; Isaiah 55:11

Signature: _Irose DeMater_

Decree Date: _June 2, 2018_

Additional Decree Details:

_____

_____

_____

_____

Daily Decree Notes:

_____

_____

_____

_____

Date the Decree Was Received: ____June 5, 2018____

Decree Testimony:

_____

_____

_____

_____

_____

_____

DAY 5

THE DREAMER'S DECREE

And it shall come to pass afterward that I will pour out My Spirit on all flesh; your sons and your daughters shall prophesy, your old men shall dream dreams, your young men shall see visions. (Joel 2:28)

I decree Your kingdom come, Your will be done, on earth as it is in heaven.

I rid myself from the leaven of the flesh and declare God's kingdom will expand like leaven.

I prepare my heart and make ready the way for the coming of the Lord. I receive the double portion and the witness of His Spirit in my life and ministry.

I call forth the Josephs—the God dreamers—and the prophets into their rightful places and positions. I declare divine alignment will yield great wealth and increase for God's people and I shall see the fulfillment of God-dreams and prophecies this year and in the years to come.

Supporting Scriptures: Matthew 6:10; James 1:21; Psalm 51:10; 2 Kings 2:9; Psalm 105:17–22

Signature: *Teresa DeMater*

Decree Date: *June 3, 2018*

Additional Decree Details:

_____

_____

_____

_____

Daily Decree Notes:

_____

_____

_____

_____

Date the Decree Was Received: June 3, 2018

Decree Testimony:
I decreed - over my Sunday school
class - they would rise up and
be who God called them to be!
They - watched you-tube on Akianna -
& Bethel kids - singing & dancing & they
received it - They saw their own gifts
and - 3 kids danced, - they led communion -
they colored w/ total contentment! Thank you,
                                        Jesus!!

DAY 6

THE HARVEST OF SOULS DECREE

Then [Jesus] said to His disciples, "The harvest truly is plentiful, but the laborers are few."   (Matthew 9:37)

I decree that I will walk in a greater passion for God's presence and a new compassion for the lost. This desire is stirred and awakened within my heart. I realize that the Great Commission is my divine destiny. I make it my purpose to unite with the fivefold ministries to reap a harvest of souls. As I reap the harvest of souls, I will walk in supernatural power with miracles, signs, and wonders following me.

I will see the harvest that is waiting on me. I will not allow another harvest to dry rot in the fields! I will not allow another generation to pass away without seeing Your glory upon Your church.

I thank You for it, Father. I decree it and receive it now, in Jesus' name.

Additional Scriptures: Matthew 14:14, 28:18–20; 1 Corinthians 1:10; Ephesians 4:11; Hebrews 2:4

Signature: _Teresa DeMato_

Decree Date: _June 4, 2018_

Additional Decree Details:

I decree that I am harmony to my husband - in response to a Word from the Lord back at Christ Life fellowship! Harmony in everything even singing voice!! :)

Daily Decree Notes:

Posted this decree on facebook! - I love to shine the Light on Facebook!

Date the Decree Was Received: June 4, 2018

Decree Testimony:

DAY 7
THE FAVOR DECREE

And Jesus increased in wisdom and stature, and in favor with God and men. (Luke 2:52)

For You, O LORD, will bless the righteous; with favor You will surround him as with a shield. (Psalm 5:12)

I decree that today is a day of favor. Favor is my portion. Just as Jesus increased in wisdom, stature (influence) and favor with God and man, so am I. I am surrounded with the shield of favor. I am favored because I favor His righteous cause in the earth.

Like Joseph, I am able to bring favor to my family and to others.

Like Benjamin, I am favored and receive five times more.

I am an heir. I am a joint-heir with Christ. I am a child of the King so I walk in His favor. The set time for favor has come. I walk in the fullness of favor. Those who receive and bless me will increase in favor.

I decree favor over my life. Favor over my family. Favor over my children and my children's children. Favor over everything and everyone I am responsible for. Favor over my relationships. Favor over my finances. Favor over my health. Favor over my church and leadership. Favor over my leaders. Favor coming in and favor going out. Favor everywhere I go, in Jesus' name.

Supporting Scriptures: 1 Samuel 2:26; Genesis 45; Genesis 43:34; Romans 8:17; Psalm 102:13, 145:16

Signature: *Susa DeMator*

Decree Date: *June - 5, 2018*

Additional Decree Details:

I decree favor with my son, Favor w/ the city for club, Favor for a life-guard, Favor w/ the Bank, Favor with the stock market, Favor w/ land lord Deidre)

Daily Decree Notes:

I have been posting & sharing these decrees and I feel the power of them everyday. Thank you Lord!

Date the Decree Was Received: June 5, 2018

Decree Testimony:

Had a meeting w/ Kathleen today and saw the fruit of wisdom taking place in her life. I also prayed with Jan today and was able to encourage her with this decree.

DAY 8

THE POWER DECREE

And you shall remember the LORD your God, for it is He who gives you power to get wealth, that He may establish His covenant which He swore to your fathers, as it is this day. (Deuteronomy 8:18)

I decree that God has given me the power to get wealth. So I will remember Him in everything I do, for He has given me everything I have and made me all that I am. In Him I live and move and have my being.

I declare and decree that God has given me the divine ability to generate wealth for the kingdom of God. Streams of income flow in and through me for God's house to be established in the earth. An abundance of strategies, finances, and resources are entrusted to me because I keep God first in all I do.

Supporting Scriptures: Psalm 112; Matthew 6:31–34; Acts 17:28

Signature: _Tresa DeMator_

Decree Date: _June 6, 2a8_

Additional Decree Details: miles –

Tanya's brother –

Sam –

Daily Decree Notes:

I had a dream about doing hair last nite, and charging people – I was coloring hair + cutting hair – and asking particular charge.

Date the Decree Was Received: June 6, 2018

Decree Testimony:

DAY 9

THE TIMING DECREE

To everything there is a season, a time for every purpose under heaven: a time to be born, and a time to die; a time to plant, and a time to pluck what is planted.

(Ecclesiastes 3:1–2)

I decree that just as the sons of Issachar understood the times and seasons so will I. I will walk in sync with heaven and know where to invest my money and time so that it yields a maximum return for kingdom advancement.

I know when and what to sow, to save, and to spend.

The Lord gives me understanding of kingdom economics so that, like Isaac, I'm able to reap a hundredfold, even in the midst of famine.

Like the four lepers I will move out in faith and will experience supernatural increase.

Supporting Scriptures: 1 Chronicles 12:32; 2 Corinthians 9:6; Genesis 26:12; 2 Corinthians 5:7; 2 Kings 7:3

Signature: _Leesa De Matto_

Decree Date: _June 7, 2018_

Additional Decree Details:

_____

_____

_____

_____

Daily Decree Notes:

_____

_____

_____

_____

Date the Decree Was Received: June 7, 2018

Decree Testimony:

_____

_____

_____

_____

_____

_____

DAY 10

THE DOUBLE DECREE

Instead of your shame you shall have double honor, and instead of confusion they shall rejoice in their portion. Therefore in their land they shall possess double; everlasting joy shall be theirs. (Isaiah 61:7)

I decree the enemy will not rejoice over me! For when I fall, I shall arise; and for my shame, I shall have double. I will endure and take my stand in the Lord.

This day I enter into possessing the double portion of God's anointing, revelation, wisdom, character, and finances.

I set my faith to lead a double portion of souls into the kingdom of God.

I know that my God shall do superabundantly above all I could ask, think, hope, imagine, or dream, in Jesus' name.

Supporting Scriptures: Micah 7:8; 2 Timothy 2:3; Ephesians 3:20

Signature: _Iusa D. Mator_

Decree Date: _June 8, 2018_

Additional Decree Details:

_____

_____

_____

_____

Daily Decree Notes:

_____

_____

_____

_____

Date the Decree Was Received: _____

Decree Testimony:

_____

_____

_____

_____

_____

_____

DAY 11

THE DOER'S DECREE

But be doers of the word, and not hearers only, deceiving yourselves. (James 1:22)

I decree that I'm a doer of the Word of God. Because I do what the Word of God says, I will have what the Word of God promises.

I decree that I am not a hearer only, I am a doer of God's Word. I look into the Word and I change what needs to be changed then continue in the truth of His Word.

My life is fruitful because I apply and abide in God's Word. I produce much fruit that remains and brings glory and honor to God.

Supporting Scriptures: 2 Timothy 3:16; Romans 2:13; John 17:17, 15:4; Matthew 7:16

Signature: _Susan DeMato_

Decree Date: _June 9th 2018_

Additional Decree Details:

_____

_____

_____

_____

Daily Decree Notes:

_____

_____

_____

_____

Date the Decree Was Received: _____

Decree Testimony:

_____

_____

_____

_____

_____

_____

DAY 12

THE GOVERNOR'S DECREE

*In that day I will make the governors of Judah like a fire-pan
in the woodpile, and like a fiery torch in the sheaves; they
shall devour all the surrounding peoples on the right hand
and on the left, but Jerusalem shall be inhabited again in her
own place—Jerusalem.* (Zechariah 12:6)

I decree that God is raising up an army of governors of praise
throughout the earth. As a governor, I take my seat with Christ in
heavenly places. I assume my delegated position, no longer looking
up at the enemy but looking down upon the enemies of the kingdom of God. I sit with Christ and laugh the enemy into derision.

As a governor, I wield praise as a weapon and execute the
judgments of the Lord. I release the sounds of heaven and, in
the name of Jesus, I tell the devil to shut up. No weapon formed
against me shall prosper and every tongue that rises against me I
pass sentence on now.

As a member of the body of Christ and His holy congress,
I pass divine legislation that thwarts the plans of darkness and
releases the blessings and promises of the Lord. I render powerless the enemy's tactics of sickness, disease, division, doubt, lack,
poverty, debt, divorce, depression, deception, accusations, curses,

and anything that tries to rise up against my life, my family, and church.

I invoke the name that's above every name, the mighty and matchless name of *Jesus*, and I enforce the divine decrees and promises of God's Word that have been ratified by His shed blood! I appropriate the provisions, prosperity, and power of Christ's will in my life and territory in Jesus' name.

Supporting Scriptures: Ephesians 2:6; Psalm 110:1; Isaiah 54:17, 61:1

Signature: _____ *Lusa DeMatti*

Decree Date: _____ *June 10, 248*

Additional Decree Details:

_____

_____

_____

_____

Daily Decree Notes:

2 Tim 1:7

_____

_____

_____

Date the Decree Was Received: _____

Decree Testimony:

_____

_____

_____

_____

_____

_____

DAY 13

THE HEIR'S DECREE

The Spirit Himself bears witness with our spirit that we are children of God, and if children, then heirs—heirs of God and joint heirs with Christ, if indeed we suffer with Him, that we may also be glorified together. (Romans 8:16–17)

I decree that I am prospering in every area of my life. I prosper because it's my heavenly Father's greatest desire for me as one of His children. I prosper because I am prospering in my soul by meditating, standing upon, and decreeing the Word of God.

God is prospering me to prosper and expand His kingdom in the earth. As an heir and joint heir with Christ Jesus, I choose to rise above a life of mediocrity and receive my rightful inheritance this day.

Supporting Scriptures: Psalm 1:2–3; Joshua 1:8; Romans 8:17

Signature: *Lusa D. Mater*

Decree Date: *June 11, 2018*

Additional Decree Details:

I found a new decree in Psalm 24:6 - This is Jacob, the generation of those who seek Him, Who seek Your face. Selah

Daily Decree Notes:

_____

_____

_____

_____

Date the Decree Was Received: _____

Decree Testimony:

_____

_____

_____

_____

_____

_____

DAY 14

THE INCREASE DECREE

So then neither he who plants is anything, nor he who waters, but God who gives the increase. (1 Corinthians 3:7)

May the Lord give you increase more and more, you and your children. (Psalm 115:14)

Of the increase of His government and peace there will be no end, upon the throne of David and over His kingdom, to order it and establish it with judgment and justice from that time forward, even forever. The zeal of the Lord of hosts will perform this. (Isaiah 9:7)

I decree that today is a day of exponential increase. I am increasing in wisdom. I decree that the God of increase is multiplying the fruit of my labor. I am increasing in favor. I am increasing in influence. My faith is increasing. My finances are increasing. My health is increasing. My relationships are increasing. My business is increasing. My church is increasing in salvations and disciples. My ability to give is increasing. My resources are increasing.

Divine doors and opportunities are increasing in my life. Joy is increasing in my life. Peace is increasing in my life. My love for the Lord and others is increasing. Faith is increasing in my life. The productivity of my life is increasing. My prayer life is increasing. My understanding is increasing. My ability to hear and know the voice of the Lord is increasing. My discernment is increasing. My spiritual eyesight, insight, foresight is increasing. Clarity is increasing in every area of my life. My heart to serve others is increasing. I am going from faith to faith, glory to glory, and strength to strength, in Jesus' name.

Supporting Scriptures: Isaiah 29:19; Luke 2:52; Ephesians 1:17–23; Luke 17:5–6; 2 Corinthians 3:18; Psalm 84:7

Signature: _Tirsa A Matu_

Decree Date: _June 12, 2018_

Additional Decree Details:

_____

_____

_____

_____

Daily Decree Notes:

_____

_____

_____

_____

Date the Decree Was Received: _____

Decree Testimony:

_____

_____

_____

_____

_____

DAY 15

THE PROSPERITY DECREE

Though your beginning was small, yet your latter end would increase abundantly. (Job 8:7)

I decree that no weapon formed against me shall prosper and that every tongue that rises against me will be proven to be false. As an heir, I pass divine legislation that silences the enemy. Every lie of lack, poverty, or insufficiency is nullified and destroyed.

The truth of God's Word propels me forward causing me to prevail in prosperity. What the enemy meant for evil, God is turning around for my good. I receive my breakthrough and walk in victory today, in Jesus' name.

Supporting Scriptures: Isaiah 54:17; Psalm 119:160; Genesis 50:20; Deuteronomy 20:4

Signature: _Tursa aMatu_

Decree Date: _June 13, 2018_

Additional Decree Details:

_____

_____

_____

_____

Daily Decree Notes:

_____

_____

_____

_____

Date the Decree Was Received: _____

Decree Testimony:

_____

_____

_____

_____

_____

_____

DAY 16

THE SOWER'S DECREE

Now may He who supplies seed to the sower, and bread for food, supply and multiply the seed you have sown and increase the fruits of your righteousness....

(2 Corinthians 9:10)

I decree God's promise to supply me with seed to sow on every good occasion. Let my tithe and giving increase and multiply in all that my field produces. I am anointed to sow into the things of God. I am a financier of the kingdom of God and I increase in kingdom economics.

Let men bless the Lord in all places of His dominion. Lord, let Your kingdom advance and be established through preaching, teaching, and healing. As a demand is placed, I am anointed to supply and to rebuke the devourer for Jesus' name's sake.

I have more than enough to sow because God is *Jehovah Jireh*—the Lord God, my Provider—my Source and Resource. I declare Isaiah 55:10 to manifest in my life—even as the rain and the snow fall down from heaven, and does not return until it waters the earth, making it to bud and flourish, that it may give me seed and bread—so it is in my life.

Let my barns and floor be full of wheat and my vats overflow with wine and oil. I prophesy that my barns are filled with plenty and my presses burst with new wine. I have the commanded blessing on my storehouse to increase, multiply, and produce lasting fruits of righteousness.

Supporting Scriptures: Malachi 3:12; Isaiah 55:10; Joel 2:24; Deuteronomy 28:8, 14:22; Psalm 103:19

Signature: _Luisa DeMateo_

Decree Date: _June 14, 2018_

Additional Decree Details:

_____

_____

_____

_____

Daily Decree Notes:

_____

_____

_____

_____

Date the Decree Was Received: _____

Decree Testimony:

_____

_____

_____

_____

_____

_____

DAY 17

THE REAPER'S DECREE

Give, and it will be given to you: good measure, pressed down, shaken together, and running over will be put into your bosom. For with the same measure that you use, it will be measured back to you. (Luke 6:38)

I decree God's promise for me to reap a continual harvest. Even as I have given, I receive blessings, overflowing with milk, honey, oil and wine.

I will reap even where I have not sown. Lead me into my land of milk and honey, a good land. The plowman overtakes the reaper in my life, and the treader of grapes, the sower of the seed, and I live in increase, abundance, and prosperity.

Let the mountains drip with sweet wine and the hills shall flow with it in my life. My gates are open continually to reap wealth.

Supporting Scriptures: John 4:36; Amos 9:13; Proverbs 8:18; Exodus 3:8; Isaiah 60

Signature: _____

Decree Date: _June 15, 2018_

Additional Decree Details:

_____

_____

_____

_____

Daily Decree Notes:

_____

_____

_____

_____

Date the Decree Was Received: _____

Decree Testimony:

_____

_____

_____

_____

_____

_____

DAY 18

THE EXPANSION DECREE

"Sing, barren woman, who has never had a baby. Fill the air with song, you who've never experienced childbirth! You're ending up with far more children than all those childbearing women." GOD *says so! "Clear lots of ground for your tents! Make your tents large. Spread out! Think big! Use plenty of rope, drive the tent pegs deep. You're going to need lots of elbow room for your growing family. You're going to take over whole nations; you're going to resettle abandoned cities. Don't be afraid—you're not going to be embarrassed. Don't hold back—you're not going to come up short. You'll forget all about the humiliations of your youth, and the indignities of being a widow will fade from memory. For your Maker is your bridegroom, his name,* GOD-*of-the-Angel-Armies! Your Redeemer is The Holy of Israel, known as God of the whole earth."*
(Isaiah 54:1–6 MSG)

I decree that today is a day of expansion. Internal expansion will bring forth external expansion of God's kingdom. I am expanding to expand the kingdom of God in the earth.

My capacity to believe is expanding. My capacity to receive from the Holy Spirit and those He leads is expanding and enlarging. My heart is expanding to care for others. My ability to reach the lost is expanding. My mental capacity is expanding. Creativity is expanding in my life and in my spheres of influence.

I decree expansion over my family. Expansion over my church. Expansion over what I've been given. Expansion over every area of my life.

Supporting Scriptures: Ephesians 3:20; Romans 5:10; Isaiah 9:7

Signature: _Juse A Mato_

Decree Date: _June 15, 2018_

Additional Decree Details:

_____

_____

_____

_____

Daily Decree Notes:

_____

_____

_____

_____

Date the Decree Was Received: _____

Decree Testimony:

_____

_____

_____

_____

_____

_____

DAY 19

THE DEBT-FREE DECREE

The LORD will open to you His good treasure, the heavens, to give the rain to your land in its season, and to bless all the work of your hand. You shall lend to many nations, but you shall not borrow. And the LORD will make you the head and not the tail; you shall be above only, and not be beneath, if you heed the commandments of the LORD your God, which I command you today, and are careful to observe them.
(Deuteronomy 28:12–13)

Owe no one anything except to love one another, for he who loves another has fulfilled the law. (Romans 13:8)

The young lions lack and suffer hunger; but those who seek the LORD shall not lack any good thing. (Psalm 34:10)

I decree I am debt free. Supernatural debt cancellation is my portion. Whatever I touch is blessed. Lack and insufficiency cannot abide in my life. Limitations of poverty are broken and the power to receive wealth is my portion, not only for me but also for my family and those in my sphere of responsibility.

My children are debt free. My grandchildren are debt free. My great-grandchildren are debt free. My church is debt free. My business is debt free. Because I am debt free, I am able to walk as a general of generosity and be a blessing to others.

Just as every debt was paid when Jesus said, *"It is finished,"* (John 19:30) on the cross, so it is in my life. I decree that I owe no man anything except to love him. I am the head not the tail. I am above and not beneath. I decree this is my Jubilee.

Supporting Scriptures: Deuteronomy 8:18; Proverbs 10:22; Leviticus 25:8–17

Signature: _____

Decree Date: _____

Additional Decree Details:

_____

_____

_____

_____

Daily Decree Notes:

_____

_____

_____

_____

Date the Decree Was Received: _____

Decree Testimony:

_____

_____

_____

_____

_____

_____

DAY 20

THE FIRE DECREE

For our God is a consuming fire. (Hebrews 12:29)

That is why I would remind you to stir up (rekindle the embers of, fan the flame of, and keep burning) the [gracious] gift of God, [the inner fire] that is in you by means of the laying on of my hands [with those of the elders at your ordination]. (2 Timothy 1:6 AMPC)

And His disciples remembered that it is written [in the Holy Scriptures], Zeal (the fervor of love) for Your house will eat Me up. [I will be consumed with jealousy for the honor of Your house.] (John 2:17 AMPC)

…and your zeal has stirred up the majority. (2 Corinthians 9:2)

I decree that the fire within me is untamable and uncontainable. I decree that a holy fire will rise within me, igniting sparks of healing and the supernatural breakthrough everywhere I go. The fire of God is impacting every person I encounter. The wild fire in my soul will cause a forest fire in my city, relationships, workplace, and nation.

I declare that through my intimacy with Christ, reverence for His presence, Word, and delegated authority, and through expectation, my fire will increase rapidly. I decree that I will not grow weary in well-doing, but I will remain fervent, because in due season I will reap a bountiful harvest for the kingdom of God. I decree that the fervency and passion behind my prayer life will stoke fervency within my sphere of influence. My zeal for the Lord and His house will stir others in their pursuit of Jesus. My fervency will connect me with the currency of heaven, therefore the attributes and fullness of heaven will overtake every other area of my life.

Supporting Scriptures: Deuteronomy 4:24; 2 Chronicles 7:1–3; 1 Kings 18:36–39; Acts 2:1–4

Signature: _Tunda aMatur_

Decree Date: _June 18, 2018_

Additional Decree Details:

_____

_____

_____

_____

Daily Decree Notes:

_____

_____

_____

_____

Date the Decree Was Received: _____

Decree Testimony:

_____

_____

_____

_____

_____

_____

DAY 21

THE ACCELERATION DECREE

Therefore say to them, "Thus says the Lord GOD: 'None of My words will be postponed any more, but the word which I speak will be done,' says the Lord GOD." (Ezekiel 12:28)

Well, tell them, "GOD, the Master, says, 'Nothing of what I say is on hold. What I say happens.' Decree of GOD, the Master." (Ezekiel 12:28 MSG)

Then the LORD said to me, "You have seen well, for I am ready to perform My word." (Jeremiah 1:12)

I decree that an anointing of acceleration is now coming and flowing in my life. Delay is dislodged and destroyed and my *"now season"* overtakes me.

The lie of the enemy of perpetual postponement of God's promises falls powerless to the ground and I move into a season of perpetual prosperity and progress. God's time twins—suddenly and immediately—hang out with me frequently and shift me into *kairos* moments and momentum.

I'm accessing, accelerating, and advancing into the abundance God has promised in every area of my life. I declare and decree, "This is my *now* season," in Jesus' name.

Supporting Scriptures: Hebrews 11:1; Jeremiah 1:11; Mark 1:17–18

Signature: _Teresa DeMatthew_

Decree Date: _June 19, 2018_

Additional Decree Details:

_____

_____

_____

_____

Daily Decree Notes:

_____

_____

_____

_____

Date the Decree Was Received: _____

Decree Testimony:

_____

_____

_____

_____

_____

_____

DAY 22

THE SUPER DECREE

*Now to Him Who, by (in consequence of) the [action of His]
power that is at work within us, is able to [carry out His purpose and] do superabundantly, far over and above all that
we [dare] ask or think [infinitely beyond our highest prayers,
desires, thoughts, hopes, or [dreams]….*

(Ephesians 3:20 AMPC)

I decree I'm moving from Delay Drive to Ephesians 3:20
Parkway!

I declare and decree that God is doing superabundantly far
over what I could ever hope, dream, or imagine!

My harvest is multiplying and overtaking me. Supernatural
increase is my portion. The plowman is overtaking the reaper. I
am increasing in wisdom and moral stature, and in favor with God
and man. I am living in the overflow of God's favor and glory.

Supporting Scriptures: Amos 9; John 10:10; Luke 2:52

Signature: _Tina Dekek_

Decree Date: _June 20, 2018_

Additional Decree Details:

_____

_____

_____

_____

Daily Decree Notes:

_____

_____

_____

_____

Date the Decree Was Received: _____

Decree Testimony:

_____

_____

_____

_____

_____

_____

DAY 23

THE _Healing_ DECREE

Write your own decree.
(For assistance, see chapter 7: Ten Keys of Decrees.)

Key Verse: _Numbers 21:9_
Isaiah 53:4

_____

_____

_____

I DECREE _____

_____

_____

_____

_____

_____

_____

_____

_____

_____

_____

_____

Signature: _____

Decree Date: _____

Additional Decree Details:

_____

_____

_____

_____

Daily Decree Notes:

_____

_____

_____

_____

Date the Decree Was Received: _____

Decree Testimony:

_____

_____

_____

_____

_____

_____

EPILOGUE

WHAT'S NEXT?

Once the decrees have been released and established, what's next? I'm so glad you asked! As Paul Harvey would say, "And now for the rest of the story!"

Let's look at Job 22:28 again and discover what comes next.

You shall also decide and decree a thing, and it shall be established for you; and the light [of God's favor] shall shine upon your ways. (Job 22:28 AMPC)

You'll decide what you want and it will happen; your life will be bathed in light. (Job 22:28 MSG)

BATHED IN LIGHT!

Do you see that? Once the decree has been made and established, God says, in effect, "And that's not all; I'm going to shine My light of favor on everything you do!" Once decided and decreed, it will happen and He will bathe you in His light. Glory to God! In other words, God will favor you so much that people will be drawn to His glory on your life.

You see, God has a vested interest in your prosperity. He not only wants you to be blessed, He also wants to establish His covenant in the earth. So get ready to shine like you've never shined before, for God is about to bathe you in the light of His glory!

ABOUT THE AUTHOR

Joshua Fowler is the apostle and lead minister of Legacy Life Church in Orlando, Florida. As a fifth-generation minister, he has a rich heritage of ministry with a great-grandfather who preached seventy years and grandfather who started two missions on a Native American reservation. From birth, Joshua travelled throughout America with his parents in evangelistic ministry.

Joshua celebrated his thirtieth ministry anniversary in January 2017. He is a sought-after national and international conference speaker and has ministered extensively in many nations around the world. Joshua is the author of five other books, including *Prophetic Praise*. He is also a gifted musician, psalmist, and a recording artist.

Joshua is the founder of GodDay.com and Shoes4KidsUSA. com. He has established churches and ministries throughout America and in other nations. Many people affectionately call Joshua "Papa" and look to him as their spiritual father in ministry. Numerous businessmen and women look to Joshua for wisdom and prophetic counsel.

Joshua convenes regional, national, and global five-fold roundtables and gatherings throughout the year, which as many as

1,500 leaders from five continents, twenty-six nations, and twenty-five states have attended.

Joshua ministers with apostolic authority and prophetic precision to equip believers to build a legacy that awakens nations and generations. He and his family live in Orlando, Florida.

joshuafowler.com

LegacyLife.org

Email: office@joshuafowler.com

Welcome to Our House!

We Have a Special Gift for You

It is our privilege and pleasure to share in your love of Christian books. We are committed to bringing you authors and books that feed, challenge, and enrich your faith.

To show our appreciation, we invite you to sign up to receive a specially selected **Reader Appreciation Gift**, with our compliments. Just go to the Web address at the bottom of this page.

God bless you as you seek a deeper walk with Him!

WE HAVE A GIFT FOR YOU. VISIT:

whpub.me/nonfictionthx

WHITAKER
HOUSE